The One-Minute
Business Writer

The One-Minute Business Writer

Arthur H. Bell, Ph.D.
and
Roger Wyse

DOW JONES-IRWIN

Homewood, Illinois 60430

ISBN 0-87094-893-8
Library of Congress Catalog Card No. 86-71317
Printed in the United States of America

1 2 3 4 5 6 7 8 9 0 K 3 2 1 0 9 8 7 6

Contents

Overview   **1**

Part One
Prewriting   **3**

Minute 1   Getting Started   **5**
Minute 2   Overcoming Writer's Block: Baseball   **6**
Minute 3   Overcoming Writer's Block: The Nudge   **9**
Minute 4   Using Active Memory   **11**
            Association. Imagery. Grouping/Organization. Spatial Ordering.
            Mnemonic Device/Language.
Minute 5   Producing Ideas   **14**
Minute 6   Finding the Words   **16**
Minute 7   Settling on a Purpose   **17**
            Decide on Your Purpose before You Begin to Write.
Minute 8   Handling the Topic   **18**
            Convert Topics to Problem Statements.
Minute 9   Creating an Outline   **19**
Minute 10   Sounding Like You   **21**
Minute 11   Preventing Logical Flaws   **24**
            Logical Error 1: Post Hoc Ergo Propter Hoc. Logical Error 2:
            Restating the Obvious. Logical Error 3: The Undistributed Mid-
            dle. Logical Error 4: Setting Up a Straw Man. Logical Error 5:
            Ad Hominem Argumentation.
Minute 12   Choosing the Right Document   **26**
Minute 13   Emphasizing YOU   **28**
Minute 14   Using Form Documents   **29**
Minute 15   Tuning Out the Editors   **30**

Part Two
Drafting   31

Minute 16   Writing the First Draft   33
Minute 17   Organizing Documents   34
            Generating an Organizational Pattern.
Minute 18   Shaping Documents   37
Minute 19   Planning Paragraphs   38
            Paragraph Length. Paragraph No-Nos.
Minute 20   Sending Early Messages   41
Minute 21   Reducing the Lard   42
Minute 22   Relating Key Points   43
Minute 23   Using Transition Signals   45
Minute 24   Mapping the Document   46
            Format Cues. Visual Cues. Verbal Cues.
Minute 25   Choosing Words   48
Minute 26   Stating the Bottom Line   50
Minute 27   Subordinating Information   52
Minute 28   Coloring Your Words   54
Minute 29   Choosing a Style   58
Minute 30   Documenting Sources   59

Part Three
Revising   61

Minute 31   Testing for Revision   63
            Test 1. Test 2.
Minute 32   Editing Quickly   64
Minute 33   Keeping It Brief   66
Minute 34   Reducing Heavy Nouns   70
Minute 35   Breaking Up Noun Clots   71

Minute 36   Using Strong Verbs   72
            A Remedy to Is/Are/Was/Were.
Minute 37   Activating Passive Verbs   74
Minute 38   Avoiding Which   76
Minute 39   Varying Sentences   78
            Repetitive Rhythm. Varied Rhythm.
Minute 40   Organizing Visually   81
Minute 41   Imprinting Your Message   83
Minute 42   Avoiding Sexual Bias   85
Minute 43   Personalizing Your Messages   87
Minute 44   Using Graphics   88
Minute 45   Creating the Package   90

Part Four
Applying   91

Minute 46   Shaping the Memo   93
Minute 47   Organizing Letters 1   94
Minute 48   Organizing Letters 2   96
Minute 49   Presenting Documents   98
Minute 50   Editing for Others   99
Minute 51   Saying No   101
Minute 52   Reading for Improvement   103
Minute 53   Creating Resumes   104
Minute 54   Writing for the Senses   107
Minute 55   Getting Feedback   109
            Prior Feedback. Feedback from the Recipient.
Minute 56   Playing Devil's Advocate   111
Minute 57   Writing for Electronic Mail   113
Minute 58   Writing with a Word Processor   115
Minute 59   Writing as a Team   116
Minute 60   Checking Your Work   118

Part Five
Writer's Toolbox: A Basic Resource for Business Writers 119

Commas Semicolons Colons Dashes Parentheses Punctuation Recap: Commas, Semicolons, Colons, Dash, Parentheses Quotation Marks Italics Apostrophes Capitalization Misplaced Modifiers Pronouns Agreement Spelling Most Commonly Misspelled Words Plurals Our Strange Language Frequently Confused Words Standard Abbreviations Numbers Research Tools for Business Folding Business Correspondence

Part Six
Sample Business Documents 151

Short Memo Long Memo (Memo Report) Sales Letter Direct Sales Letter 1 Direct Sales Letter 2 Claims (Complaint) Letter Adjustment Letter Credit Approval Letter Credit Denial Letter Letter Responding to a Problem Collection Letter: First Notice Recommendation Letter Resignation Letter Instructional/Procedural Writing Application Letter Chronological Resume Functional Resume Progress Report Format for the Long Report Omniform 3000 Proposal Detailed Cost Presentation in Proposals Short Report

Index 191

OVERVIEW

We offer 60 one-minute lessons in the art of business writing. Then you'll find the Writer's Toolbox, a brief summary of grammar, mechanics, spelling, and usage. Finally, you can review sample memos, letters, reports, proposals, resumes, and instructions in the Sample Business Documents.

Good writing!

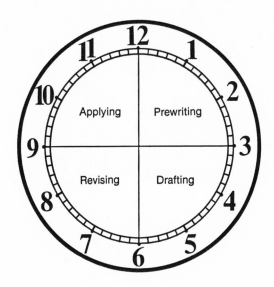

Part One

Prewriting

Minute 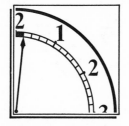 1

Getting Started

Read the following Declaration of Independence for business writers:

1. Past problems with writing, whether in school or on the job, mean *nothing* about your ability to learn to write well. Don't psyche yourself out.
2. Writing is a craft like carpentry or knitting. With the right tools, techniques, and a little time, you can write like a pro.

Overcoming Writer's Block:
Baseball

You're stuck. Every sentence you begin to write is wrong, wrong, wrong.

Here's one way to get going. First of all, turn your emotions of frustration and self-pity into healthy anger and determination. In effect, quit babying yourself. The writing task before you may not be fun—but that's all the more reason to tackle it and get it done.

Second, play this little game. Draw a set of bases as illustrated below.

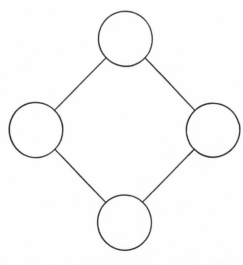

Now force yourself to fill each of the bases with an idea related to your topic. If you're working on Employee Absenteeism, for example, the bases might be filled as follows:

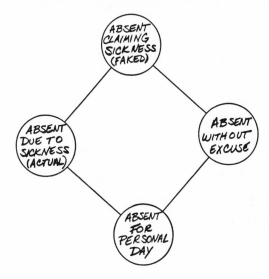

Notice what's happened as you've filled the bases? Some of your main players are on the field. Go ahead and rearrange them if you wish. Which should be on first? Which on second? What are your background ideas in the outfield? Who's doing the pitching? Within a matter of minutes you have a wealth of ideas before you.

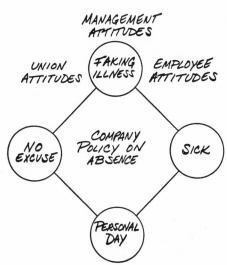

Now look over the playing field and make a list. What should you discuss first? What second? The models in Minutes 46, 47, and 48 can be helpful in shaping your list. But you probably won't need anyone's model. You'll see the commonsense order of ideas for yourself.

Here's a list—the Agenda List—for Employee Absenteeism. Notice that reminders for support material have been jotted alongside many of the items in the list:

- Company policy (outdated, often ignored).
- Causes for absence:
  Sick.
  Faking.   Employee attitudes
  Personal.
  AWOL.
- Union attitudes (see contract).
- Management attitudes.

Minute  3

Overcoming Writer's Block: The Nudge

So you're not into baseball? If you gave the technique in Minute 2 an honest effort and came up dry, break your writer's block by playing the "nudge."

It works like this. Ask yourself each of the eight questions in the "nudge." Fill in your problem statement wherever a blank appears. As ideas occur to you (and they will!) jot them down for use in your writing.

• THE NUDGE •

Nudge 1: When I think of ＿＿＿＿＿＿＿＿＿ , one thing comes to mind more than anything else.

Nudge 2: People disagree about ＿＿＿＿＿＿＿＿＿ . Some feel that (fill in. . .). Others feel that (fill in. . .).

Nudge 3: It's helpful to divide ＿＿＿＿＿＿＿＿＿ into three (choose your number) parts:

Nudge 4: Understanding ＿＿＿＿＿＿＿＿＿ depends on your viewpoint. Here are two common viewpoints:

Nudge 5: We can grasp ＿＿＿＿＿＿＿＿＿ more clearly by comparing it to (make a helpful comparison. . .).

Nudge 6: Certain people are especially affected by ＿＿＿＿＿＿＿＿＿ . Here's why:

Nudge 7: We can't really understand ＿＿＿＿＿＿＿＿＿ without knowing a little about its background.

Nudge 8: The best thing that can be said about ＿＿＿＿＿＿＿＿＿ is. . . . The worst thing that can be said about ＿＿＿＿＿＿＿＿＿ is. . . .

If you've played the "nudge" with some energy, you've probably filled your page with strong ideas for writing. Now arrange those ideas (using the hints in Minute 9) as a working outline for your first draft.

Minute  4

Using Active Memory

Your writing really begins "upstairs," in your mind. The pen, typewriter, and the various denizens of the beep—word processors, electronic letters, videotex—merely record it for others to read.

The "nudge" and "baseball" help you remember what to write about a particular subject. But in order to remember you must first store the information in your memory banks. Unless you plan on referring to notes on everything you write, you must be able to memorize information. A wise man once said, "You can't recall the past when it's past recall."

So, learning a few simple memory techniques will save you hours of research. Let's suppose, on the way to work, you overhear this:

> You know, Bob, I just read a fascinating article about transportation 50 years from now. Planes will be able to travel at 4,500 miles per hour, almost seven times the speed of sound. And you should see some of the strange designs these planes will have: ring wings, twin fuselages, forward-swept wings. There's even going to be a cargo plane that's wing shaped.

Later on you decide to write a memo to your department, but you didn't catch the name of the article, or what magazine the article came from. Later on you wish you did because, as Director of Research and Development at Advanced Aero Designs, you want your people to know about designs of the future.

You could have used any of five memory strategies (or a combination) to remember the important bits and pieces of the conversation:

- Association.
- Imagery.

- Grouping/organization.
- Spatial ordering.
- Mnemonic devices/language.

Association

In the association method, you link information to whatever fact, event, action, sensation, emotion, or idea that comes to mind. That way, all you have to do is "dial" previously stored information to remember the story.

To recall 50 years, 7 times the speed of sound, and 4,500 miles per hour, you might link "50" with your age, "7" with the soft drink 7UP, and 4,500 with your favorite novel *Fahrenheit 451*. Then, to recall the facts, picture yourself drinking a 7UP and reading *Fahrenheit 451* on your 50th birthday.

Imagery

The imagery method involves free associating images; for instance, to remember airplane designs, you could associate a ring with the ring wing, scissors for the forward-swept wings, and a boomerang for the wing-shaped cargo plane.

Grouping/Organization

Group and organize the information in whatever form suits you. For instance, you might categorize the information this way:

Stats	*Plane Design*
7 times the speed of sound	Ring wings
50 years from now	Twin fuselages
4,500 miles per hour	Forward-swept wings

Spatial Ordering

Picture the futuristic aircraft landing at the nearest airport. Spatially order them one after the other in the sky and imprint the scene in your mind. You've just used the same memory muscles that allow you to remember street directions.

Mneumonic Devices/Language

Mneumonic devices use sounds, letters, and language to help you recall hard-to-remember information. For example, to remember the wing designs, take the first letter of *forward-swept*, *twin fuselage*, and *ring*. The initials "FTR" can then be linked to President Roosevelt, or FDR. Just think of FDR and the initials "FTR," meaning forward, twin, and ring.

Not only mneumonics but language can be used to remember the wing designs. Take the words *ring*, *twin*, and *forward* and make a sentence that makes sense to you. For instance, you could say, "I look *forward* to the church bells *ringing twice* each day."

Producing Ideas

Writing can be as spontaneous as a novaburst or it can be as slow as a stalagmite formation. Your mind is a veritable wellspring of original ideas. So let's tap into it.

The "nudge" and "baseball" are fine for most people, but let's suppose you want your freedom. All right, let's free associate using the constellation method. Here's how it works: Think of your ideas as shining stars. Start with any thought. Draw a circle around it.

It's the center of your first bright idea. Any related idea that pops into your mind then becomes a planet. Throw in a moon here and there if you want. Pretty soon you have a whole solar system of ideas available for writing (see page 15).

You come across another idea that's unrelated or too big to fit in this solar system. Start another system and another until finally you have a whole universe of ideas. Relate and position the planets and stars to each other.

You will find that your thoughts fall into a meaningful order on the page. Use that order to create a working outline like those described in Minute 9.

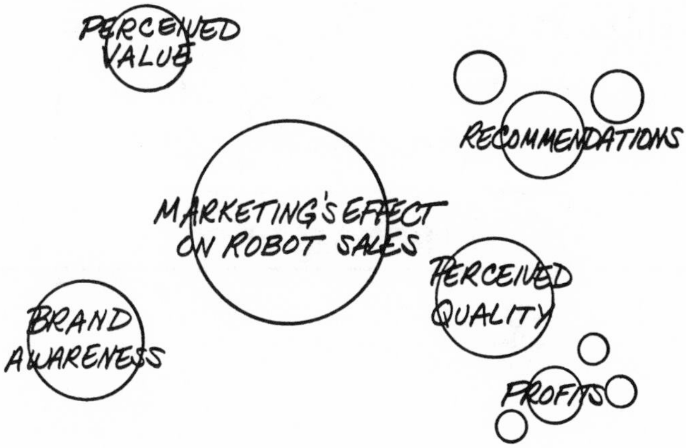
PERCEIVED VALUE
RECOMMENDATIONS
MARKETING'S EFFECT ON ROBOT SALES
PERCEIVED QUALITY
BRAND AWARENESS
PROFITS

Minute  6

Finding the Words

The actual words you need to express your ideas are already assembling themselves in your mind—"on the tip of the tongue," we say. Learn to *listen* for those words. Picture yourself describing your ideas to a friend. What words come to mind? What do you "hear" yourself saying? Those are the words you want for your rough draft.

Usually they come from the mind in small packages—phrases. Don't be discouraged, therefore, if you can't capture an entire sentence at a time from the mind. At the same time, don't be satisfied with plucking only a word at a time from the active mind. Listen for groups of words, then combine them on the page into meaningful sentences.

Minute  7

Settling on a Purpose

What are your words trying to accomplish? Once you decide, you'll know which words to choose. Here are some choices:

- To inform my readers—I'll arrange my material in a clear, logical way. I want them to say, "Oh, I see now."
- To persuade my readers—I'll describe the problem and possible solutions as convincingly as possible. I want my readers to say, "You're right."
- To motivate action—I'll show my readers the benefits of taking recommended action. I want them to say, "Let's do it."

Many business documents are a blending of two or more purposes. To keep your own goals solidly before you as you write, take 20 seconds to jot down your purpose on a three-by-five-inch card. Set it in front of you. Use it as a rudder to keep you on course.

DECIDE ON YOUR PURPOSE BEFORE YOU BEGIN
TO WRITE.

Minute  8

Handling the Topic

"Henderson, I need a brief report on employee absenteeism."

Employee absenteeism. You have your topic from the boss. Are you ready to write? Of course not.

Topics are for encyclopedia writers, not business writers. Convert your topic to a *problem statement:*

Topic ——————————→ Problem Statement
Employee Absenteeism —→ Absenteeism—A Growing Problem
at WRT, Inc.

Notice that mere topics just lie there in the mind. There's so much to say that you don't know where to begin. "Corn Prices in Nebraska." "Geological Formations." Who *could* write well about such topics? They don't suggest a path for development to the writer.

But problem statements do. We can describe *what* the facts are about the problem of absenteeism. We can show *how* it affects production. We can discuss *why* employees are absent so often. If the boss desires, we can offer recommendations to decrease the problem.

Get the point? Call it the "DALLAS" approach to topics: find a problem ("J.R.'s car is wired with a bomb"), and the mind is hooked. Thinking and writing become easier because we know what to *do* with problems: *solve* them. We don't know what to do with topics.

CONVERT TOPICS TO PROBLEM STATEMENTS.

Minute  9

Creating an Outline

Just as a meeting needs an agenda to keep on track, so you'll need a working outline to keep ideas flowing in a smooth and orderly way.

What luck have you had with the old sixth grade form of outline?

I. Major point
  A. Subpoint
     (support)
  B. Subpoint
     (support)
  C. Subpoint
     (support)
       . . . and so forth

If it still works for you, great. Use it to arrange the ideas you've generated from the "bases" or the "nudge."

But for many of us, the sixth grade outline just doesn't work well for writing. If you, too, have trouble translating this outline into actual sentences and paragraphs, try the following method of organization.

Fill the big boxes (they look suspiciously like paragraphs, don't they?) with your main ideas. Order those ideas so that they make your point in a logical, persuasive way. Then go back to fill in the smaller boxes with supporting ideas, details, and examples. Of course you can draw more boxes anywhere you need them to fit your material.

• BOXES AS AN OUTLINE FOR WRITING •

As an example, the first few boxes have been filled in with ideas we might use for our report on the problem of employee absenteeism.

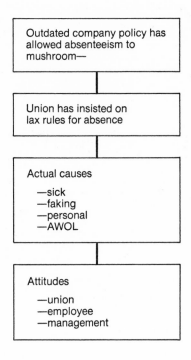

Sounding Like You

Have you noticed that you've never experienced "talker's block?"

"Hey, Frank, how's your golf game?"

"Well . . . uh . . . Damn, I have talker's block. Maybe I can answer you after I stare at the wall for awhile or visit the refrigerator."

It never happens. Why? Because we all express ourselves clearly and easily *when we let ourselves speak naturally.* To write with similar ease, use your natural voice. "Speak" your way along in your writing, talking to your reader in natural, common-sense language.

In short, find your "voice." Notice in the following example how Jane Richland, an insurance executive, gives up the institutional voice for her natural voice. Which would you prefer to read in a memo crossing your desk?

Jane Richland in an institutional voice:

It is incumbent upon me to bring to your attention the policy established by this company with regard to the smoking of cigarettes in offices occupied by more than one person when that person or persons are self-identified nonsmokers. . . .

Jane Richland in her natural business voice:

By company policy, don't smoke in shared offices without the consent of all officemates.

Needless to say, Jane Richland prefers her natural voice. She can write quickly and painlessly because she says what she means and means what she says. Her readers like her natural voice. They feel they're in touch with Jane through her words, not an institutional impersonality.

Most of all, her readers like the fact that Jane's natural voice gets to the point and doesn't waste words. A two-page institutional memo turns into a one-paragraph memo in a natural voice. (Jane's company is pleased as well: that one-paragraph memo is faster to read, type, transmit, reproduce, and file.)

If you're stuck in a stiff, unnatural voice, follow these four suggestions to break free into your natural business voice:

- Ask yourself, "What am I trying say?" Literally speak your answer aloud and listen to the words you use. Don't fall back into the awkward, stiff language of the institution. Use your spoken words as a guide to a natural, direct way of expressing your ideas.
- Forget "the way the boss writes." If he or she uses ridiculously obtuse words and constructions, that's no reason for you to follow suit. Perhaps the boss can afford to be obscure. You and I can't. We earn our livings and achieve our goals by getting to the point in a clear way.
- Picture your readers' faces as you write. How will they react to your words? Do you see them frowning? Scratching

THE WALL STREET JOURNAL

STEIN

"As far as I can tell, he's out to lunch." *Pepper . . . and Salt*

heads? Rubbing eyes? If so, scrape off the heavy makeup of obscure, stiff language from your writing. Say it simply and make them smile.

- Laugh a little at your own pretensions. Who are you trying to sound like? Is the person speaking in your writing the same person you saw in the mirror this morning? Are you playing the business version of Dr. Jekyll and Mr. Hyde in your choice of voices? Be yourself.

Minute  11

Preventing Logical Flaws

Most documents in business are structured on the basis of what we would call "commonsense" logic. For example, a writer supports major points with evidence not because he or she has had a course in Aristotelian logic, but instead because such a method is a common way to prove a point. We make this point for a reason: clear common sense is one of the writer's best assets in constructing a business document. If you've got it, use it!

But even writers with an abundance of commonsense can occasionally stumble into logical errors. Here are five logical potholes to avoid in your writing:

Logical Error 1: Post Hoc Ergo Propter Hoc

Forget the Latin if you wish, but remember the error: claiming that X was *caused by* Y just because X occurred *after* Y. You wouldn't argue, for example, that flood damage to your company in May occurred because the weather bureau predicted rains some days earlier. An earlier event is not necessarily the cause of a later event.

Logical Error 2: Restating the Obvious

Avoid rephrasing in the second half of a statement the terms of the first half of the statement. Don't be caught, for example, in this logical snafu:

"This company has built a solid reputation by taking steps to let the public know we exist." (Notice that "reputation" and "know we exist" are the same thing. We've proven only that A = A.)

Logical Error 3: The Undistributed Middle

If all managers are women, and you're a woman, does that prove that you're a manager? Common sense says no. Yet many business documents make this crucial logical error. Can you spot the error in this advertisement?

All quality homes use plaster, not drywall, for walls and ceilings. At Ace Construction, we specialize in plaster. You can be assured that an Ace home is a quality home.

No. Even if all quality homes use plaster, that doesn't mean that using plaster guarantees you a quality home. Try to mentally revise the advertisement before looking at the repaired version that follows.

All quality homes are plaster, not drywall, for walls and ceilings. At Ace Construction, we build quality homes and therefore use nothing but plaster for walls and ceilings.

Logical Error 4: Setting Up a Straw Man

One easy but illogical way to attack a position is to fashion a "straw man" or falsified and simplified version of the position, then to destroy that fabrication. Watch the process at work in the following example:

Those who want to move company headquarters to Las Vegas are interested only in gambling. I can prove that gambling inevitably lowers production rates, employee morale, and hence company profits.

The writer has reduced the opponent's position to the false and simple grounds of gambling. By attacking the gambling issue, the writer illogically claims to be addressing the question of whether or not to move the headquarters.

Logical Error 5: Ad Hominem Argumentation

In this logical error, the writer attacks the people behind an idea, not the idea itself. Here's an example:

Your attorney has advised you not to sign the contract for three reasons. But consider your attorney: do you know that he defended two of the Watergate conspirators?

Notice in ad hominem argumentation how the issue shifts illogically away from the merits of the question to the merits of the men or women involved.

Minute  12

Choosing the Right Document

Choosing the right document is like choosing the right weapon. Sir Lancelot wouldn't use a jousting pole to slay a dragon. So, you too must be careful to choose the right weapon, or "write" weapon, to convince the reader.

"Collins, we need to revamp our benefit structure. Give me a plan." You heard the boss. What do you do? Reach for the Alka Seltzer? Maybe, but it won't clarify the assignment. Chances are your boss isn't sure what document you should write either. In this case, you could choose any document. It all depends on your purpose.

Given the purpose, the following chart shows which document to choose.

| | **Purpose** | | |
	Suggest *Prompt*	*Explain* *Inform*	*Analyze* *Persuade*
Short	Short memo	Short report	Short proposal
Long	Long memo	Long report	Long report
	Informal	*Formal*	*Formal*
		Formality	

Turn to the Model Documents section of this book for examples of each document. As the chart illustrates, *memos* are informal documents. They're the everyday documents passed back and forth between business people. Memos get the ball rolling. In our example, Collins could write a memo to offer some suggestions informally.

Of course, if Collins chose to put a little weight behind his words, he'd choose a formal document. To explain the different plans available, he might choose to write a *report* on it. In the report, he could make recommendations. The report formalizes his thoughts and places them under greater scrutiny.

If Collins chooses to analyze and compare the different plans available with an eye toward proposing a new approach, he would write a formal *proposal.* In it, he would analyze the merits of each plan and propose a comprehensive approach to the problem. Proposals are persuasive devices, more so than any other document. In it, Collins would go a step further than the report by trying to persuade the company to *act* upon his comprehensive approach to the problem.

Minute  13

Emphasizing YOU

When we write, we draw together what we think and then set it down. Right?

Wrong—at least for many business situations. When we simply disgorge our own preoccupations, we're in danger of boring and alienating the reader. Why should he or she *care* about our musings?

A more appropriate version of business writing goes like this: we call to mind our thoughts and then recast them in ways relevant to the needs and interests of our readers. That's the YOU perspective.

Notice in the following pair of examples how a self-obsessed ME perspective gives way to a more appropriate YOU perspective.

Me: I'm proud to open my sixth BIG BOY store in Glenville, adding to my growing business and my personal fortune.

You: Another BIG BOY store comes to Glenville to serve your needs. You'll find the best in. . . .

Minute  14

Using Form Documents

Borrowing is always easier than creating. When faced with a writing task, many writers feel the strong temptation to reach into the file for a "form" of some type to follow. Here's a bit of advice on such borrowing.

First, recognize that you are not developing your own expressive powers. If, indeed, career mobility depends on the ability to write quickly and effectively, you may be slowing your own professional development by a steady reliance on form documents.

Second, you may miscommunicate. Few situations in business avail themselves of the "cookie-cutter" approach to writing. Your reader may have special needs and sensitivities that aren't treated at all in the form document you select.

Third, you may waste time. Remodeling a form document to suit your purpose may actually take longer than writing the message you intend.

Evaluate form documents carefully before considering them a "solution" to the problems involved in writing. On some occasions, they can prove to be just what the doctor ordered. On others, they may be part of the illness, not the cure.

Minute  15

Tuning Out the Editors

One of Jackie Gleason's more famous lines from *The Honeymooners* series was his elephant-like bellow, "SHUT UP!" Writers, too, have to learn to say "shut up" to the many editors (internal and external) that interfere with the drafting process. Consider three of these editors:

- **The teacher editor.** These voices remind you of all the writing mistakes you've made in the past. "You can't do it because you just don't have the talent," they say.
- **The professional editor.** These voices remind you of how much is at stake. Other people will read your words. You'll reveal what you do and don't know. You might make embarrassing errors. "We'll find out that you're not so hot," these voices say.
- **The text editor.** This voice knows certain things about grammar, mechanics, spelling, usage, and style. It speaks up to challenge you on each word, phrase, and sentence. "Shouldn't you do it *this* way?" the text editor asks again and again.

"SHUT UP" is the appropriate response to these editors during the drafting process. As a writer, you have to let yourself write freely. There will always be time for correction and revision later. But for now, learn to tune out the editors. No famous pianist plays a masterpiece while thinking of all the mistakes he or she could be making. In the same way, learn to "go with the music" while drafting. Don't let niggling editors spoil your act of creation.

Part Two

Drafting

Minute 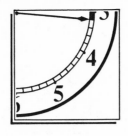 16

Writing the First Draft

You're worried. You've invested time in getting your determination up, generating ideas, and creating a solid outline. But where are the words of your report?

Do not worry. Every minute you've spent in prewriting planning will save you ten minutes of agony in the actual writing of your document.

Now get to the task, following these suggestions:

- Keep your purpose in mind (remember your three-by-five-inch card?).
- Work in a comfortable place.
- Minimize distractions.
- Set aside a chunk of time. Don't try to write by the installment plan.
- Let it all hang out. Don't be too hard on yourself about spelling errors, awkward phrases, or odd-sized paragraphs. Those can all be fixed later. Go for it!

Minute 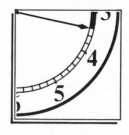 17

Organizing Documents

The most common criticism of business documents has nothing to do with grammar, spelling, or punctuation. "It's disorganized," the boss says. "Clean it up!"

Understand, first, that there are two kinds of organization possible for a topic or problem. Intrinsic (or "built-in") organization occurs whenever the topic comes with its own internal ordering of parts. In writing about dental coverage, for example, you may choose to follow the built-in pattern of organization already worked out in the insurance company's plan description: "Hygienic Visits," "Fillings," "Removals," "Oral Surgery," and so forth.

But more often, you must come up with—and impose—your own system of organization on a topic or problem. How do you spawn an organizational pattern? Just as important, how do you know what kind of organizational pattern fits your material?

Generating an Organizational Pattern

Bear in mind that an organizational pattern is just a tool to accomplish a goal. There are no "preordained" patterns of organization proper for all documents at all times. You have not only the right as a writer but also the duty at times to design your own organizational approach: a series of steps that takes readers exactly where you want.

Here are three situations from actual business experience and the organizational patterns that grew out of them. Follow these examples as a guide to creating your own patterns of organization.

• EXAMPLE 1. JUDY CHRISTCALL AT MILLWORTH GRAIN SUPPLY •

The Situation. Judy must write a general promotion letter to readers she doesn't know. Millworth wants to expand its business to the North Valley.

An organizational plan for Judy's promotion letter:

Paragraph 1: Here's a problem we can both relate to.

Paragraph 2: Here's the Millworth answer.

Paragraph 3: Here are benefits to you rising out of business with Millworth.

Paragraph 4: Here's our earnest, friendly invitation to visit our mill and warehouse, or to call for a bid on our services.

• EXAMPLE 2. JAVIER RAMIREZ AT WESTERN FINANCIAL ASSOCIATES •

The Situation. Western Financial has been acquiring properties encumbered with "creative" financing. In his memo, Javier directs purchasing agents to avoid such acquisitions.

An organizational plan for Javier's memo:

Paragraph 1: Here's my directive, in case they don't read any further.

Paragraph 2: Here's my explanation and interpretation.

Paragraph 3: Here are some important exceptions.

Paragraph 4: Here's what to do if they have questions.

• EXAMPLE 3. FRIEDA WALTERS AT EXPRESS ELECTRONICS, INC. •

The Situation. The vice president of operations has asked Frieda to write a report with recommendations on delays in the 704 Project, a microcomputer being developed by Express.

An organizational plan for Frieda's report:

I. The present status of the 704 project

The boss wants to know where things stand.

II. Background

The boss needs to know what led to the present situation.

III. Evaluation of development delays

The boss will want to understand exactly why and how the project was delayed.

IV. Alternatives

The boss will want to review several possible routes of action.

V. Conclusions, with recommendations

The boss will want to know which alternative I think is best, and why.

Organizational plans of this sort pay dividends to the writer:
- You know what areas you'll need to research.
- You stay on track in writing the report.
- You provide a structure so that your reader stays on track in reading the report.

Minute 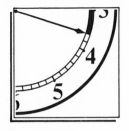 18

Shaping Documents

Sculptors have a gift: they are able to "see" the shape of their eventual artworks even when beginning to chip away at the marble for the first time. They know what to leave and what to eliminate because they have a vision of what will be.

Shrewd business writers can develop that same gift. They can have a mental "snapshot" of what the finished document can and should look like even before writing begins. Follow four steps to develop this ability:

1. **Decide upon length in advance.** Do you want a one-page memo? A three-page proposal? Write *toward* that goal instead of letting the eventual length simply "happen."
2. **Decide upon placement.** Where on the page should your major points fall? Remember that the beginning of the page—the strong slot—catches the eye of the reader most of all.
3. **Decide upon emphasis.** Which sentences, words, or phrases should be highlighted by boldface or underlining? Which ideas or examples should receive less emphasis by visual subordination (using inset margins and perhaps bullets)?
4. **Decide upon visual highlights.** What graphics will enrich your presentation? Where do they belong? Minute 44 will advise you on the choice, use, and placement of graphics.

Minute  19

Planning Paragraphs

If you're confused about what goes on within the organization of paragraph, it's no wonder. We've all heard lots of bad advice:

Wrong: "Tell 'em what you're going to say, say it, then tell 'em what you've said." (This advice leads to long, awkward, repetitious paragraphs. Don't heed it.)

Wrong: "Stay with one paragraph until you're ready to move on to a totally new idea." (Paragraphs following this wrong-headed notion often span more than a page.)

Instead, think of your paragraphs from your readers' point of view. Readers look at your paragraphs as your chance—

- To make a point and discuss (or support) it.
- To break up the page into visual packages.

The following structure can be found at the heart of most business paragraphs. Use it if you're searching for a way to order your sentences within a paragraph:

Topic sentence: Here's my point in one sentence.
Expansion, if necessary: Here's what I mean. . . .
Discussion, support: Here's why. . . .
Wrap-up: Here's the bottom line.

Notice how this pattern works in the following example.

Even though their union has been negotiating for a four-day workweek, few employees want to work more than eight hours per day. A four-day workweek, by general agreement, would mean ten-hour days. Most employees, especially those with children, do not want to leave home before breakfast or arrive home after the dinner hour. Employees themselves should be polled by the company before further negotiation regarding the four-day workweek.

What about very short paragraphs? They can be quite useful in business writing if not overused. (Too many short paragraphs on a page, for example, force the reader to try to tie them all together into one meaningful package. Readers don't want to work that hard.)

Use a short paragraph when you want an idea to stand out, perhaps in introduction or summation. Here's a short paragraph from a business letter:

In summary, the Wolf Creek development shows every promise of meeting its sales goals by September 1987.

In the context of the whole letter, that sentence contains very good news indeed. The writer wants the good news to stand out, and so visually separates it from other words by using a short paragraph.

Don't use a short paragraph to contain a supporting point that should properly appear together with its main idea.

Paragraph Length

How long should a paragraph be? Let observation be your guide. Notice the length of paragraphs in annual reports, especially those written by professional writers. Few paragraphs, you will find, exceed seven or eight sentences without good reason (a complicated argument, an extended list, and so forth). In most cases, paragraphs hover around four to six sentences, yielding perhaps three paragraphs or so to a typed, double-spaced page.

Paragraph No-Nos

Don't let a paragraph fill an entire page.

Don't place two or more short paragraphs next to one another.

Don't bury your central point in the middle of your paragraph.

Don't change topics inside a paragraph.

Don't try to make all of your paragraphs the same length.

Minute  20

Sending Early Messages

Readers want to grasp your message *early* in the paragraph. Don't be shy or coy. Don't wander through unnecessary introduction or histories. In a direct way, state your point as early in a memo, letter, or report as possible.

Especially during hectic business days, harried readers may not have the time, energy, or inclination to read more than a few sentences of your document. Make sure that those few sentences work for you by communicating your message.

• EXAMPLE OF EARLY MESSAGING IN A LETTER •

Dear Mr. Klein:

Yes, I would be pleased to speak to the Lions Club at 7:30 on January 4.

(instead of "I have received your letter requesting me to speak. . . .")

• EXAMPLE OF EARLY MESSAGING IN A MEMO •

To: Bill Victors

From: Cheryl Wilson

Subject: Company Picnic

Date: February 9, 1986

Bill, we need your help in reserving Memorial Park for our company picnic on May 7.

(instead of "As you know, this company holds a picnic for its employees each May. . . .")

Reducing the Lard

Here's a brief experiment. Glance at the following number for a few seconds, then cover it with your hand. Try to repeat the number from memory:

14111982111098765432166654342

The point? Simply that long strings of numbers—and words—can boggle the mind. We quickly forget the beginning of the string as we move on and on and on.

But what happens when the string is broken up into shorter units? Try the same memory experiment on the same list of numbers:

1 411 1982 11 10 9 8 7 6 5 4 3 2 1 665 4342

These numbers have twice the impact on our memories because we're able to see them for what they are: distinct packages of meaning, not a confusing conglomeration.

Notice how the short words/short sentences version of the following message is easier to read and remember:

• LONG WORDS, LONG SENTENCE •

Prior to the initiation of his employment with this company, it was Frank Henderson's objective to serve in the management capacity of a corporation specializing in the production of cables for use with computers.

• SHORT WORDS, SHORTER SENTENCE •

Before beginning work with this company, Frank Henderson wanted to manage a computer cable company.

Minute  22

Relating Key Points

Are these equations correct or incorrect?

$$
\begin{array}{rcr}
5 \quad 2 & = & 3 \\
7 \quad 4 & = & 11 \\
8 \quad 2 & = & 4 \\
9 \quad 3 & = & 27
\end{array}
$$

Somewhat confused? Who wouldn't be? We need to know the *relations* between these numbers (+, −, and so forth) before we can make mathematical sense out of them.

In the same way, readers can't easily make sense out of your sentences without some signals showing how they are supposed to relate.

Here's a list of Relation Signals you should post like traffic signs throughout your business paragraphs. Show your readers exactly where you're headed in your writing—and where you want them to follow.

therefore	if . . . then
however	also
first, second, third	in addition
nevertheless	furthermore
by contrast	for example
in comparison to	for instance
	such, this, these

In the following example, the first paragraph does not make use of Relation Signals. The second does. Notice that the second paragraph is easier to read and understand.

• PARAGRAPH WITHOUT RELATION SIGNALS •

The parking lot outside Plant Nine looks like a trash heap. The lots surrounding the other plants remain tidy throughout the week. The difference can be explained by the bright orange trash barrels located every 100 feet on the clean lots. The barrels give employees a place to deposit trash. The bright orange color serves as a visual reminder not to dump trash onto the lot itself.

• PARAGRAPH WITH RELATION SIGNALS •

The parking lot outside Plant Nine looks like a trash heap. By contrast, the lots surrounding the other plants remain tidy throughout the week. This difference can be explained by the bright orange trash barrels located every 100 feet on the clean lots. These barrels give employees a place to deposit trash. Furthermore, the bright orange color serves as a visual reminder not to dump trash onto the lot itself.

Should every sentence begin or contain a relation signal of some type? No. Just as a highway can be cluttered with too many traffic signs, so a paragraph can become unreadable with too many relation signals. Use these markers with discretion to guide the reader at any point where he or she may misunderstand your direction.

Minute  23

Using Transition Signals

You've made your point in a paragraph. You're ready to move on—but how does the reader know?

First, you show that you're changing directions by beginning a new paragraph. Second, you take time to include a Transition Signal—"on the other hand," "by contrast," "viewed from another perspective," and so forth—at the beginning of your new paragraph.

Here is a list of useful transition signals. As with relation signals, use them whenever you feel that the reader may misunderstand your intent.

in the same way	this kind of
at the same time	consequently
simultaneously	in spite of
just as. . .	from another point
instead of	of view
as we have seen	finally

In the following example, the highlighted transition signal clearly announces that the writer is changing directions.

. . . rejecting management's insistence on fewer breaks during the workday.

The union did not, *however,* challenge the notion that lunch hours can be reduced to 45 minutes at management's discretion.

Minute  24

Mapping the Document

We've talked about transitions and signs for the reader. Now let's take a look at the whole signpost landscape. Cues come in the three basic forms: format, visual, and verbal.

Format Cues

Format cues vary with the format; for instance, for reports the following cues preview your points:

> Cover
> Table of contents
> Abstract
> Letter of transmittal
> Abstract
> Overview
> Headings
> Body
> Bibliography

(See model document "Format for the Long Report.")

Visual Cues

Visual cues orient the reader. Used sparingly and appropriately, they can be effective.

> Pictures, graphs, and charts
> Print:
>   Typeface
>   Underlining

Numbering
Arrangement:
  White space
  Indenting
  Bullets

Verbal Cues

Once readers know the format and see the cues, they have to be oriented from sentence to sentence. The following cues do this:

Transitions
Conjunctions
Repetitions

Minute  25

Choosing Words

Which words should you choose? This question has concerned poets, pundits, and business people alike since men and women began etching their initials in stone tablets thousands of years ago.

Everyday you see business people grappling with words. The credit department calls the understated credit an "unfortunate circumstance"; you call it a mistake. Your boss writes a memo stating, "It was decided that..." when everyone and his brother knows *who* decided.

For business documents, three questions influence word choice:

- What is my purpose?
- Who is the reader?
- What is the situation?

In the following example, Peter Windborough must "explain" a serious problem to the vice president with a memo. Here's the situation:

Windborough, account executive at Pacific International, mistakenly traded the Brookhurst account below margin (margin required to cover potential losses). "Don't worry," he said, "the funds are on the way." The trade lost and the money never arrived.

Here's the memo Peter has begun to write:

> As you are aware, the Brookhurst account lost beyond account margin by $7,231 this week. After repeated requests, the Brookhursts refuse to meet the shortfall.
>
> This situation was due to a (an) _____ .

Now we're at the critical juncture of the memo. Should Peter use the word *mistake, oversight,* or the term *unfortunate circumstance*? Let's take a look at the variables:

Purpose: To save his reputation and job.
Reader: Boss's boss, who likes "straight talk."
Situation: To explain what happened.

Which should he choose? In this case, he should probably use either "mistake" or "oversight." The first conveys "straight talk" but calls to question Peter's competence. The second still hints at a mistake and takes responsibility, but it says to the reader, "It could have happened to anyone." The vice president would probably find the third, "unfortunate circumstance," totally evasive.

Of course every situation differs, but using purpose, reader, and situation as your guide, you'll choose the right word.

Minute  26

Stating the Bottom Line

"Daddy, are we there yet?" The whine isn't coming from the back seat. It's coming from your readers.

They want to know, with good reason, if you've gotten to your point. If they're holding a longish report in hand, they have every reason to ask their question. Do you expect them to wait until page 16 for your "bottom line" judgments? Or will you sum up your major points as you go along? If so, how are they to know?

Answer your readers' need for "bottom line" summaries by pausing often to draw matters to a point. Key introductory words and phrases can be used to alert the reader to a "bottom line" statement. Here are six to include in your writing:

- In short.
- In sum (or in summary).
- Here's the point.
- So far we've determine that. . . .
- In conclusion.
- To bring all to a point.

• EXAMPLE OF BOTTOM LINE STATEMENTS IN A LETTER •

To sum up, we're eager to participate in the 1988 national convention. Count on our best efforts.

Sincerely,
Bob White

• EXAMPLE OF BOTTOM LINE STATEMENT
IN AN INSTRUCTION •

In short, take whatever commonsense measures are necessary to make sure that no one walks on newly installed tile for at least 48 hours after installation.

Minute  27

Subordinating Information

You've followed the rules. First find the true subject and follow it with an action verb. Start quickly and keep it short whenever possible. But what happens when you want to add extra information and don't want to write another sentence? That's when you need to know how to subordinate information.

Let's consider the following sentence and subordinate information:

Sentence	Subordinate Information
Our group will meet	Conference room
	Next Tuesday
	5:00 P.M.

You have three places to subordinate information:

- Before the subject.
- Between the subject and verb.
- After the verb.

Here's what each looks like:

1. In the conference room at 5:00 P.M. next Tuesday, our group will meet.
2. Our group, in the conference room at 5:00 P.M. next Tuesday, will meet.
3. Our group will meet in the conference room at 5:00 P.M. next Tuesday.

Which is grammatically correct? The answer is all three, though alternative 2 is certainly awkward. Which should you use in business writing? It depends on the situation, information, and desired affect. If your reader should see the information early for emphasis, choose alternative 1. Or to get quickly off the mark, choose alternative 3. Alternative 2 can be useful in providing variety to your sentence rhythms: "Jackson [the subject], long a respected employee with this company, finally retired [the verb].

You can also pack information into more than one of the slots in the sentences. Notice the combination of alternatives 1 and 3.

Next Tuesday at 5:00 P.M., our group will meet in the conference room.

Minute 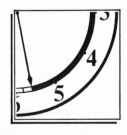 28

Coloring Your Words

You've formulated your ideas using the "Bases" or the "Nudge." You know what to write. But what words should you choose, and what reaction will the reader have to them? What tone should the document take? What you're wondering about is style.

Though your printer, typewriter, stylus, or pen may use black ink, your words suggest many different tones. Like an artist, you have many stylistic colors on your palette, the document. Gradations aside, let's stick to four basic colors—no magentas, please—just red, yellow, orange, and blue. Then perhaps you can decide which color style to use.

Using the basic qualities of these colors, we can describe the four styles. Red tones suggest a forceful, imperative style. Yellow suggests a passive, impersonal style. Orange connotes a bright, "colorful" style, and true blue gives you an honest, personal style.

The following example shows four ways Janice Kendall could respond to a letter inviting her to serve on the Board of Urban Development. Each conveys basically the same message with a different style.

• INVITATION •

Dear Janice,

I recently submitted your name as a possible member of the Board of Urban Development for the Piedmont area. And the board voted yes!

We're a growing community and could use you on the board. Please say yes.

Barbara Jenkins
Board of Urban Development

• RED STYLE •

Dear Barbara,

I cannot say yes to your invitation. Quite frankly I am surprised that you extended it in the first place. Here are my reasons for rejecting your offer:

- Conflict of interest.
- Dissatisfaction with your committee's views.
- Time constraints.

I will talk to you soon. In the meantime, find out if I can serve in an advisory capacity to the committee.

Janice Kendall
Real Estate Developers, Inc.

• YELLOW STYLE •

Dear Barbara,

It is my whole intention to be of the most cooperative nature whenever possible, but at this time, perhaps it would be best for me to turn down your most gracious offer.

Along with time constraints and the tendency not to agree with all of the members of the board, the most compelling reason why I cannot accept the invitation is because I am an officer of Real Estate Developers, Inc.

Of course, like always, staying in touch is the best course of action. In the meantime, it would be best to see if I could serve in any other capacity.

Sincerely,

Janice Kendall
Real Estate Developers, Inc.

• ORANGE STYLE •

Dear Barbara,

Thanks for the invite, but you should know better, my friend! I can't be a member of the board and "vice pres" over here. Sure wish I could, though.

Talk to you soon. Let me know if I can help in any other way.

Sincerely,

Janice Kendall
Real Estate Developers, Inc.

• BLUE STYLE •

Dear Barbara,

Thank you for inviting me to serve on the Board of Urban Development. I can think of three reasons why I should not.

First, my serving on the board would represent a conflict of interest. You can understand that my current position would influence my decisions. Thus, I could not serve the community and my own cause.

My other two reasons are lack of time and fundamental differences with some board members.

I'm really flattered that you thought of me. Please stay in touch, and if I can be of any help, let me know.

Best wishes,

Janice Kendall
Real Estate Developers, Inc.

Which color you choose, of course, depends on taste. It's probably best to use blue whenever possible. Bear in mind, though, that each situation may call for a different stylistic color. In fact, in most situations, you'll probably mix the colors on your palette, the document.

Minute 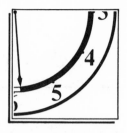 29

Choosing a Style

Is there one divine business style? Of course not. Even the advice in this book against a heavy, ambiguous style must sometimes give way to the situation at hand.

Consider the dilemma of a company executive, for example, who is asked by a reporter to comment on the company's liability in a recent chemical spill. A short, terse answer—"No comment"—may arouse hostility. Yet a frank, sincere answer—"We probably have a great deal of liability in the matter"—may be legally and professionally disastrous. What to do?

Learning to change styles to meet situations is an extremely valuable business skill. The executive faced with the dilemma described above chose to "fog" the question through somewhat obtuse, ambiguous language:

> While it is impossible at this time to make a full assessment of the unfortunate incident to which you refer, I can say that the company has obtained the services on an independent review agency of the government to assist it in evaluating both the causes and the ramifications of the incident.

Is such guff successful? It depends upon the occasion. In this case, the obtuse statement bought time for the executive and the company. The real answer could come later in a carefully worded and legally reviewed press statement.

Remember that "good business style" like a "good personality" is really a bouquet of different styles, all ready to serve as the situation demands.

Documenting Sources

A reasonably thorough treatment of the many footnote and bibliographic conventions is beyond the scope of this book. When preparing notes or a bibliography, use any of the following resources for your reference:

Campbell, William, and Stephen Ballou. *Form and Style: Theses, Reports, Term Papers.* 4th ed. Boston: Houghton Mifflin, 1974.

U.S. Government Printing Office. *A Manual of Style.* New York: Gramercy Publishing, 1986.

Modern Language Association of America. *MLA Style Sheet.* New York: Modern Language Association of America, 1980.

The University of Chicago Press. *The Chicago Manual of Style.* 13th ed. Chicago: University of Chicago Press, 1982.

Turabian, Kate. *A Manual for Writers of Term Papers, Theses, and Dissertations.* 4th ed. Chicago: University of Chicago Press, 1973.

Part Three

Revising

Minute 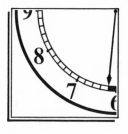 31

Testing for Revision

After finishing your document, suppose you're not sure whether it really requires a rewrite. Two quick tests can determine whether to rewrite or not to rewrite.

Test 1

Take the first line of each paragraph and use it to make a topic outline or list. Does it make sense? Reorganize and reorder the list until you have a logical argument. Then go ahead and rewrite the document.

Test 2

Choose ten sentences at random and determine the average number of words. If the average is over 16, consider rewriting. Professional writers use this measure—"Sweet 16"—to appraise the readability of their work.

Should each of your sentences number 16 words? Of course not. Continue to write a balance of short and long sentences that *average* 16 or less words.

Minute  32

Editing Quickly

Your report is a mess. The boss wants it later this morning. You've got good ideas, but you've obscured them in a tangled mess of prepositions, dangling modifiers, and convoluted phrases. What should you do?

Not to worry. Your ideas are sound, so make them *sound* good! Uncap your magic marker. Here's a quick way to make the content jump off the page:

• PART I •

1. Mark the nouns.
2. Mark the verbs.
3. Circle the prepositions.

• PART II •

1. Find the true action—make it active.
2. Find the true subject—put it up front.
3. Rephrase prepositional phrases.

The following passage illustrates this method:

Acquisitions of materials and services is accomplished via negotiations between buyers and sellers in an ethical, business-like and competitive environment. Negotiations require effective communications and imply a willingness of parties to reach a satisfactory agreement on matters of mutual concern in acquisition of supplies and services.

Here's the rewritten passage:

> Buyers and sellers should negotiate for materials and services in an ethical, business-like, and competitive environment. The two parties must communicate to transact business.

Notice that the paragraph shrunk? It's no wonder with all the nouns and prepositions strewn throughout the original. Lean lightly on nonsubject nouns, adjectives, and prepositions and your sentences will come alive. You'll find a beauty in the beast after all.

Minute  33

Keeping It Brief

Add it all up:

- Writers can write more quickly using word processing.
- Modern copy equipment can duplicate pages faster.
- Electronic mail allows users to distribute messages to thousands of receivers.
- Disk storage allows documents to be recalled and reprinted with ease.
- Data bases make millions of pages accessible for review and reproduction.

What does it add up to for you in the years ahead? Much, much more reading. If your in-basket is already brimming with memos, correspondence, catalogs, reports, and newsletters, you may wilt at the thought of twice or three times as much paper flowing to you for reading.

The only white knight on the horizon is Brevity. Already, by executive order at Alcoa, Ford, Lockheed, and elsewhere, documents are automatically limited in length. Many CEOs flatly refuse to read memos of more than a page.

If being brief were easy, we would all practice it already. Woodrow Wilson was asked how long it would take him to prepare a ten-minute speech. "About two weeks," he answered. And how long for an hour speech? "About a week." How long for a two-hour speech? "I'm ready right now," he responded. In a similar vein, Pascal quipped to a correspondent, "I would have made my letter shorter, but I didn't have time."

What are the keys to concise but complete writing? You already hold some of them from earlier lessons: short words, short sentences, well-planned paragraphs, early messages, and bottom line statements.

Now add three more specific techniques.

1. Establish the approximate length of your document *before* you begin to write. Once you've set your length, make it your goal to fit all you have to say into that limit.
2. Use *positions of emphasis* with skill. The beginning of each sentence provides you with one position of emphasis. Notice in the following example how the writer has used a position of emphasis for important content words, not weak phrases like "it is" and "there is":

Three telephone repair centers serve this business community. (Instead of "There are three telephone repair centers that serve this business community.")

Another position of emphasis occurs at the beginning of each paragraph. Readers are especially hungry at that point to know what you're trying to say. Satisfy their hunger by giving them what they want: important words and concepts that get to the heart of your message.

In the following example, notice the power of the position of emphasis at the beginning of the paragraph:

Forceful, sincere sales messages can help you achieve your personal and financial goals in this company.

A final position of emphasis can be found at the conclusion of each paragraph. Readers want to discover there the "so what?" to all you've been saying. In other words, they're looking for a summary or "bottom line" statement of some kind. You can make your point powerfully and briefly by using these positions with skill.

In this final example, a brief message is nevertheless complete by a skillful use of all the positions of emphasis described above.

Integrity often costs this company short-term profits—but never long-term success. Tell the truth to clients at all times. Those who don't want to hear the truth will choose to do business elsewhere. Those who do want to hear the truth about their investment ideas will become our best clients.

3. Finally, keep your messages brief by considering the attention span of your reader. We would all like to believe that the world stops when our letters and memos arrive. Hardly. Writers would be humbled, in fact, if they could observe the reception their documents receive from even friendly readers.

Often the sentences you've slaved over are given a glance or a scan, then set aside. "Did you read my report?" we ask. "I had a chance to look at it briefly," the reader responds.

If we had only known just *how* briefly we would have made the document much shorter. Be realistic, therefore, about what your reader wants from you. "Ars longa, vita brevis," runs the old Latin advice: "Art (including the art of writing) is long, but life is short."

The Reformer Martin Luther admitted that he never managed to say the entire Lord's Prayer without having his attention drift to other subjects, often against his conscious will. Your reader, too, has much to think about. Make your written message a morsel, not a whole side of beef. (History hasn't been kind to verbose writers. In commenting on Milton's *Paradise Lost*, Alexander Pope jibed, "No man would wish it longer.")

• THE LONG AND SHORT OF IT: A VERBOSE MEMO AND A BRIEF REWRITE •

To: Shirley Faulkner

From: Eric Towelson

Subject: Maintaining an adequate level of desk supplies

Date: March 30, 1986

It has come to my attention, specifically by the memos to me from several employees, including my own secretary, that the supply room has not been adequately stocked with such common office requirements as pencils, pens, erasers, letterhead stationery, envelopes, mailers, tape, and other items incidental to the functioning of this company.

By this memorandum I am asking you to review the present inventory to determine adequacy levels of stock in the item categories mentioned above. While I do not ask you to make a formal report to me on this matter, I do ask that you call me to inform me of any problems in either the acquisition or distribution of office supplies.

To: Shirley Faulkner

From: Eric Towelson

Subject: Inadequate supplies

Date: March 30, 1986

Several employees have complained that desk supplies aren't available. Please check on our inventory of common office supplies, then call me with a status report.

Minute  34

Reducing Heavy Nouns

You can spot them right away—those blimps of the dictionary that float on the page:

> The usefulness of the previous enhancement has proven beneficial to the attractiveness and profitability of the product.

Many of the flags are flying on our word blimps: -ness, -ment, -ial, and -ability. Throw in -tion, -sion, -ance, and a few others to produce truly unreadable business prose.

Almost all blimp nouns smother action. "To attract" becomes "attractiveness," "to profit" becomes "profitability," and so forth. Thank goodness for the human race that "to make love" hasn't been smothered into "lovability." We wouldn't be here to complain.

Converting heavy nouns to more readable prose involves two steps:

1. Find the action at the heart of the heavy noun. Sometimes, as illustrated below, the action may use a different root word than the heavy noun.

Heavy Noun	*Action Translation*
I have a responsibility concerning	I care about
In my judgment . . .	I think

2. Determine who or what in your sentence performs the action you've rescued from the heavy noun. Rewrite your sentence according to WHO does WHAT to WHOM.

Breaking Up Noun Clots

Three or more nouns in a row can delay and distort meaning. Who knows (or cares) what a "university examination policy review procedure" is or does? Meanings trip one over another.

Break up noun clots as illustrated in the following examples:

1. Make some nouns into verbs.

   Noun clot: Please bring me the seminar evaluation report summary.

   Revised: Please bring me the report summarizing the seminar evaluation.

2. Insert prepositions.

   Noun clot: His basic problem was a self-image estimation inadequacy.

   Revised: His basic problem was a low estimate of his self-image.

3. Leave out unnecessary words.

   Noun clot: Nederbahm forgot to include the convention preparation materials modules.

   Revised: Nederbahm forgot to include the preparation modules for the convention.

Minute  36

Using Strong Verbs

What's wrong with the following sentences? The words are spelled correctly. No grammatical errors occur. Yet the sentences just lie there—dry, institutional, lifeless.

> There is to be an assessment of the hiring process by personnel experts.
> It is the purpose of their review to determine the successfulness of present procedures that are used by us in hiring computer specialists.

Ugh. Do you want to attend the review sessions, based on this prose? Do you want to read the report that inevitably will grow out of the review sessions? Of course not.

Of the many villains in this sample, "is" in all its disguises ("are," "was," "were," "seems to be") leads the pack. What's wrong with using "is"?

1. You've used up the verb for your sentence. Any remaining action (like "assess" or "succeed") sink into awkward noun forms ("assessment" and "successfulness").
2. You've probably caused yourself a bout with writer's block. The easy beginning "There is . . ." gives you the feeling that you're underway only to stop you in your tracks when you realize you've said nothing. There you sit, trying to come up with words that follow from "There is. . . ."
3. You've missed your chance to give orientation to your reader. He or she, in approaching your sentences, simply wants to know "who is doing what to whom?" When readers bog down in meaningless words like "It is . . ." and "There is

. . ." (and the words that inevitably follow), they brand your writing "slow" and "hard to follow."

A Remedy to Is/Are/Was/Were

Rephrase your sentences by answering this question: "Who is doing what?" Even inanimate subjects (like "profit sharing") can perform quite lively actions:

Profit sharing benefits all employees. (A marked improvement over, "There are benefits to all employees from profit sharing.")

Notice in the first example our star, "profit sharing," comes first in the sentence (the position of emphasis) and actually gets to do something on stage ("benefits . . ."). In the version using "is," the star appears last.

Professional writers for such magazines as *Fortune*, *Forbes*, and *Business Week* use strong verbs in most of their sentences. You should too. Find an "is" sentence in your own writing and ask the key question, "Who is doing what?" In answering that question, you'll usually find the true subject and true action at the heart of what you had intended to say.

In each of the following rewrites, notice the energy and conciseness wherever strong verbs replace is/are/was/were:

No: The president's plan is to undertake the remodeling of company headquarters.

Yes: The president intends to remodel company headquarters.

No: The main problem with telephone service at this company is that static can be heard too often on the line, especially during important long-distance calls.

Yes: Static on the line interferes with good telephone communication at this company, especially during important long-distance calls.

Activating Passive Verbs

Was my vacation heard about by you? Several good slopes were skiied down by us, and a peak was climbed by us. In all, fun was had by us.

Does this language sound a bit backward to you? Didn't the writer mean to say "Did you hear about my vacation? We skiied ..." and so forth?

Certainly that's the natural way of saying it. Why, then, in business do we accept these equally backward constructions?

A meeting will be held by project managers at 2:00 P.M. The Thompson account will be discussed by them, and recommendations will be arrived at for review by management.

Say what?

As a general rule, write in the active form, not the passive form. Tell your reader WHO did WHAT to WHOM. When you use the passive form, you risk three forms of misunderstanding:

1. Readers think that the first word in the sentence is the subject. Only later in the sentence do they figure out that the beginning word receives the action instead of sending it.

   No: The rules were broken often by seasoned employees.
   Yes: Seasoned employees often broke the rules.
   No: The final calculations were made by Mira Smith.
   Yes: Mira Smith made the final calculations.
   (Notice where the emphasis falls in the active forms.)

2. The true actor in your sentence can disappear entirely. Your boss, let's say, receives a glowing report about your work unit: "Production quotas were exceeded by 22 percent."

But who gets the raise based on this report? You and your fellow workers? No—you weren't even named in the sentence. Here's what the boss should have read:

Workers in Unit Six exceeded production quotas by 22 percent.

3. Your writing sounds lifeless in the passive form. No sportswriter would get far with "The homerun was slammed by the catcher." No business writer should bury a sense of action and energy under the camouflage of passive forms.

• EXAMPLE OF PASSIVE FORM CONVERTED TO ACTIVE FORM •

Passive: Receipts for all business-related meals are required by the accounting department.

Active: The accounting department requires receipts for business-related meals.

Avoiding Which

Using "which" is an understandable temptation. We want to connect up our ideas in a business document. After announcing one idea, we simply link it to the next by "which":

Cloverton Dairy pasteurizes all its milk products, which. . . .

But what are we linking here? "Milk products?" The fact that the dairy pasteurizes its milk? You can't tell—and therein lies one problem with "which." The word glances back to previous meanings in the sentence, but often it's only a glance. We're temporarily confused. Here are both meanings of "which" in examples:

"Which" referring to "milk products":
The Cloverton Dairy pasteurizes all its milk products, which are sold primarily through supermarkets.
"Which" referring to the act of pasteurization:
The Cloverton Dairy pasteurizes all its milk products, which guarantees them a triple A rating by the Health Board.

A second reason to avoid "which" when possible has to do with reader patience. Face it: reading business documents can be hard work. The last thing a reader wants to see after working through a longish sentence is a tagalong "which" promising more words to come.

Notice when you reach a "which" after many words in a sentence that you know what you're in for: not one or two more words, but a whole passel. In computer terms, your buffer is already full to the brim with data—and now an impertinent "which" comes along auguring more work. No thanks!

Avoid "which" (when possible) by the following techniques:

1. Try an "-ing" word to replace "which."

   We located the part which had been the cause of the problem.

   (becomes)

   We located the part causing the problem.

2. See how the sentence reads when omitting "which" entirely.

   He forgot to send a response to the order which was received from Seattle.

   (becomes)

   He forgot to send a response to the order from Seattle.

Varying Sentences

It's a high compliment when someone says to you, "Your writing really flows. I like reading it." What do they mean by "flows?"

We don't have many good terms to express that meaning. The person probably means to say that the rhythm of your sentences has interesting variety—fast here, slow there, balanced here, imbalanced for effect there. Luckily, perhaps, you've never taken a class in creating such effects. Your "ear" for language told you how a sentence in context ought to sound even before you had settled on the exact words. You had a "feel" for the sentence.

A truly professional business style depends upon that intuitive sense of rhythm and flow. See if you can hear how the first passage falls into trite, stale rhythms while the second comes closer to the "flow" feeling:

Repetitive Rhythm

Sales personnel should read all manuals with care. The manuals contain information about all product lines. These details can prove useful when talking to clients. Large orders often depend on knowing products in detail.

Varied Rhythm

Sales personnel should read all manuals with care. Why? First, the manuals contain all the answers about product lines. Knowing these details can make or break sales. Even the largest orders often stand or fall depending on the sales person's knowledge of products.

To vary the rhythms in your own writing style, try to mix in some sentence types that you may not now be using. Listen for the effect and emphasis they create.

Type 1: Sentences with "-ing" and "-ed" Phrase Beginnings. Examples are:

Reaching 65, Muriel decided to retire.
Placed by himself in a quiet office, Herb doubled his production.

Type 2: Sentences that "Break" in the Middle and Seem to Begin Again. Examples are:

Muriel reached 65 last week, but she had no thought of retiring.
Herb requested a quiet office; soon his production had doubled.

Type 3: Sentences with Phrases Inserted Between Subject and Verb. Examples are:

Muriel, reaching 65, decided to retire.
Herb, working for the first time in a quiet office of his own, was able to almost double his production.

Type 4: Sentences with a Colon or Dash Near the End for Emphasis. Examples Are:

Muriel knew her retirement was near on that fateful day: her 65th birthday.
Herb now knew the secret to doubling his production—his own quiet office.

Most of your sentences will continue to begin with the subject, move to the verb, and then to the object ("Harry hit the ball"). That's as it should be. But the basic subject-verb-object pattern gets monotonous when overused. Vary it by mixing in some of the sentence types above.

THE WALL STREET JOURNAL

"It's from the IRS. They say they're going to huff and puff and blow our tax shelters down." *Pepper . . . and Salt, April 30, 1985.*

Minute  40

Organizing Visually

Even after you have established your pattern of organization and have checked for logical errors, your business document can look disorganized. "Well," the writer may be tempted to respond, "simply read the document and you'll find out it's quite organized."

There's the rub. Readers who judge a document to be disorganized in appearance may never read it at all. Or, if they do read on, they do so with a negative mindset that affects their judgment of issues in the document.

Here are three ways to give your document the "look" of professional organization. Needless to say, these techniques cannot and should not take the place of solid organization on the level of thought. Working together, both logical and visual organization can create the effective documents you want to write.

1. Set off major divisions within the document by short headings.

    This technique is common in reports and proposals, but it can also be valuable in longer memos and letters. See examples of memos that use headings effectively in the Model Documents supplement.

2. Inset lists and parallel points.

    The memos in the Model Documents section demonstrate what a relief such inset portions can be to the eye. Just as an umbrella covers whatever is beneath it, so the major point in this memo visually umbrellas the inset points.

Note, by the way, that the writer has made each of the points *parallel* in form. If the first begins with a verb ending in "-s," then all others in the list will also. Similarly, if the first item is a noun phrase ("eight cases of lubricant"), then all other phrases in that list must also be noun phrases.

3. Make generous use of white space.

Your margins and interior spacing let the reader know that you understand visual emphasis. You consciously set off important sections of the document by surrounding white space. Readers appreciate such white space because it gives them a chance to perceptually relax for a moment (white space requires no work!) before reading on.

Word processing has opened new horizons for writers who want their work to impress visually as well as rationally. Different fonts, character sizes, colors, border trims, and graphics are now available for most popular word processors. These enhancements can be overdone, of course, to produce a cute and frilly document not at all acceptable in business. But used with skill, they can be additional nonverbal communicators—silent influencers—guiding your reader's impression of your document.

Imprinting Your Message

Etch-a-sketch on your reader's mind. You've played the game before, but as a business writer, you want to indelibly sketch your message on the reader's mind. Consider this sentence:

Recommendation: In essence, it is most preferable to, and I say this with all due respect, accomplish a move to a new location, somewhere in the vicinity of Irvine or thereabouts, perhaps a little north but definitely in Orange County. The time we need to implement this plan is negligible.

Who could remember the contents of that message? Very few people, indeed. It's hard to remember. That's because memorable sentences are:

- Short.   (They are short and unambiguous.)
- Concrete.   (They give concrete images.)
- Active.   (They use the active tense.)
- Associative.   (They have an associative quality.)
- Understandable.   (They are instantly understandable.)

The list proves its first point. Keep it short and give the information *up front*. Unless you have an elephant's memory you'd probably have trouble remembering the same items in parentheses.

With these qualities in mind, let's rewrite the sentence: Recommendation: "We should move to the Irvine area." That's it— *short* and to the point. Notice how this sentence identifies the subject "we" and provides a *concrete* action, "move." Memorable sentences often follow the pattern *who does what*.

Besides being short, concrete, and active, memorable sentences *associate* images; they tell a story. The first sentence in this message, "Etch-a-sketch on your reader's mind," associates imprinting messages with the game Etch-a-sketch. Metaphorical language (even clichés), specific nouns, and descriptive adjectives, used sparingly, can increase impact.

Last but not least, memorable sentences must be *understandable*. Writers should jettison all ambiguities and simplify the message for a longer lasting impression. Who could make head or tail out of "The time we need to implement this plan is negligible"? Does the writer mean it won't take long, or there's not much time to do it? Instead, the message should read "We have little time to implement this plan" or "We must act immediately." Memorable messages always let you know where you're going.

Remember, the window to the mind is very small. Your message must shine brightly in the right direction to get through.

Minute  42

Avoiding Sexual Bias

He says, she says. Which should you choose?

Most business writers, male and female, choose male subjects. This tendency reflects traditional male/female roles. You'd like to get around it, but how? Let's suppose you've written an ad for a new promotional writer:

> Candidate will develop brochures to support marketing efforts in advanced technology. He will interview engineers and marketing manager to gather data and material for graphics. In addition, he must organize material, write copy, and work with artists to develop layouts.

In this case, you could substitute "he or she" or even "you." As an alternative, you could eliminate the subject altogether in the second and third sentence:

The promotional writer will perform the following:

1. Develop brochures. . . .
2. Interview engineers. . . .
3. Organize materials. . . .

How else do you avoid being a male or female chauvinist? First take a different attitude. Think of your colleagues and officemates as business persons, not men or women. Instead of "He must document his hours worked every week," you could write using one of these techniques:

- Employees must document their hours   (plural).
- Hours worked must be documented   (passive tense).
- An employee must document hours worked (avoid pronoun).

- You must document hours worked   (you pronoun).
- He or she must document hours worked   (he or she pronoun).

The key is to hide gender. Substitute nouns, "you," "we," or "he or she" for the single pronoun "he" or "she." Remember that business writing is the one place where sex *should* take a back seat.

THE WALL STREET JOURNAL

"In seeking a female executive to join our management team, Ms. Whitsock, we've reached unanimous agreement that you're our man." *Pepper . . . and Salt, October 29, 1985.*

Minute  43

Personalizing Your Messages

There may be good reason for an impersonal, even sterile, tone in a few technical documents. For most business writing, however, you should try to sound like what you are—a living, breathing human being.

This is not to say that feelings must gush out of your business writing. Remember the difference between sentiment (natural, appropriate feeling) and sentimentality (overinflated feelings used for manipulative purposes).

Three Ways to Personalize Your Messages

1. Use your reader's name in your text.

   Bob, we should also consider shifting the tax burden from the Pasadena property to the Los Angeles leasehold.

2. Mention your own feelings and inquire about your reader's feelings.

   Though I can't put my finger on it precisely, I have an uneasy feeling about hiring McCoy. What are your feelings?

3. Tell not only *what* you are doing but also how you *feel* about what you are doing.

   All of us at Wilson Technical Design are proud to send along to you the finished prototype.

Personal messaging invites the reader to be equally personable in return messages. That natural, human exchange lays important groundwork for solid business relations.

Using Graphics

Due to inflation, a picture is now worth far more than a thousand words. Even the simplest chart or graph can be thought of as a picture to stimulate your reader's thinking and clarify your message.

Here are five important "Do's" for using graphics:

1. Do select the right kind of graphic for your use. If you are trying to demonstrate a trend, for example, use a line chart or bar chart (where the upward or downward direction of your data will be most apparent). If, on the other hand, you're trying to demonstrate proportion or distribution, use a pie chart or segmented bar chart (all illustrated on the following page).

2. Do place charts and graphs *on the same page* as the words that refer to them. Nothing maddens a business reader more than paging back or ahead to discover what a chart is supposed to mean.

3. Do place brief, clear captions beneath charts and graphs.

4. Do surround *every* chart or graph with words. Try to lead in to the graphic by referring specifically to what you want the reader to observe: "Notice in the following chart how profits began to climb after 1982. . . ." Similarly, lead out of the graphic by referring briefly to what the reader was supposed to observe: "This sudden rise can be attributed to. . . ."

5. Do keep your charts and graphs as simple as possible. The beauty of a graphic is its ability to convey major impressions and relations in easy form. Don't detract from that beauty by too many lines on a line graph, too many segmentations on a bar chart, or too many divisions in a pie graph.

• EXAMPLES OF USEFUL GRAPHICS •

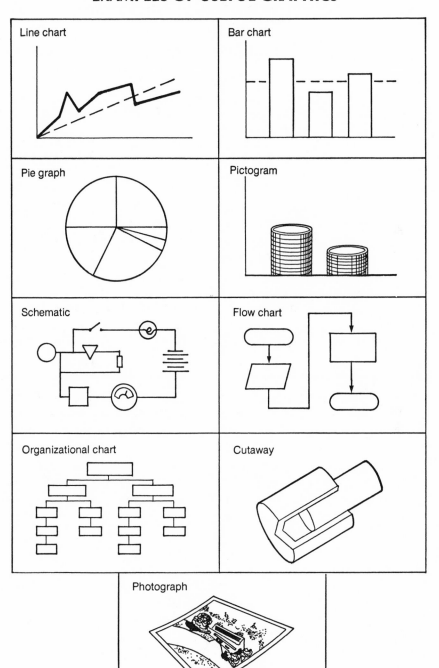

Minute  45

Creating the Package

As Marshall McLuhan observed, "the medium is the message." Applied to the concerns of business writing, the *total impression* your document makes is a large part of "what it says."

Writers should consider, therefore, the peripherals that often accompany written communications. In the case of a promotional letter, for example, does it matter if you attach a glossy brochure to the letter and mail them together in a quality envelope? Does the impression made by your letter change? Of course. The reader is influenced to look upon your words with a much more positive mindset—and hence can be persuaded or informed more easily by your words.

In the case of a proposal or report, you may want to consider such peripheral influencers as professional binding, typesetting, or accompanying materials (catalogs, supplements, related readings, and so forth).

The goal is to "think *package*" in developing business documents. Don't trust your words alone to create your intended effects. Make use of all the influencers at your disposal to surround your words with support.

Part Four

Applying

Shaping the Memo

Memos are extremely popular in present business practice because they are so easy to write. Simply follow these guidelines:

1. Begin with the traditional block opening:

   To:
   From:
   Subject:
   Date:

2. Your subject line should convey what the memo is about in the fewest words possible ("Plans for the September meeting").

3. The body of your memo can follow this order of development:

   Paragraph 1: Here's my message.

   Paragraph 2: Here's explanation, interpretation, or additional information.

   Paragraph 3: Here's specifically what I want you to do.

4. Place your initials after the "From:" portion to indicate that you have approved the typed version of the memo. Don't sign the memo as you would a business letter.

5. In longer memos, use headings to help the reader key in on major points. See the Model Documents section for examples of memos.

Minute  47

Organizing Letters 1

Of the many letters used in present business practice, six are most common:

1. Sales (promotion) letter.
2. Recommendation letter.
3. Application letter.
4. Claims letter.
5. Adjustment letter.
6. Collection letter.

The first three of these are discussed in this Minute, the final three in the next.

Sales, recommendation, and application letters all try to persuade the reader to take a recommended course of action. As such, they are based on the *reader's needs*. Before beginning to write any of these letters, therefore, ask yourself what the reader really wants and needs. How can you arrange your argument to meet those needs?

Following your consideration of needs, experiment with the following recipes in developing your own persuasive approach to your reader:

• A RECIPE FOR THE SALES LETTER •

Paragraph 1: (A short paragraph.) Grab their interest in a way related to your topic (a question? interesting fact? headline?).

Paragraph 2: Describe your wares. What are you selling?

Paragraph 3: List specific benefits. What can your product or service do for them?

Paragraph 4: Give specific directions. How can they get your product or service?

Paragraph 5: (A short paragraph.) Express your eagerness to serve their needs. You may also want to thank them and include a final "bonus" message, if appropriate. Avoid the cloying techniques of junk mail, with its insensitive "hard sell."

• A RECIPE FOR THE RECOMMENDATION LETTER •

Paragraph 1: Express your pleasure in recommending the person.

Paragraph 2: Tell in what capacity you've known the person and generalize about his or her qualities and performance.

Paragraph 3: Choose a specific strength or two for emphasis. Support your opinion by citing facts or stories about the person.

Paragraph 4: Conclude with a general, enthusiastic summary statement about the person. Offer further information if it will be helpful to the evaluator.

• A RECIPE FOR THE APPLICATION LETTER •

Paragraph 1: Mention that you are pleased to apply for the position at hand. Name that position so there can be no confusion.

Paragraph 2: Point out that you have enclosed your resume. Mention one or two highlights from the resume that may be particularly interesting to the reader.

Paragraph 3: Conclude by stating your strong interest in an interview. Include information on how the reader can reach you.

Minute  48

Organizing Letters 2

Claims, adjustment, and collection letters share a "hard edge." Most have to do with problems of some kind, often involving disputed performance or unpaid accounts. The goal in each of these letters is to communicate persuasively and effectively without resorting to (or provoking) anger. We avoid anger for one good reason: it does not lead to productive business relationships.

• A RECIPE FOR THE CLAIMS LETTER •

Paragraph 1:   Tell what happened. Rehearse the facts as you know them.

Paragraph 2:   Tell what you want done. Be specific about the solution you think will resolve the matter.

Paragraph 3:   Offer to be part of the solution by giving cooperation in some form. This concession on your part, however small, will go far toward motivating the reader to grant your claim.

Paragraph 4:   State a "starter-step"—some specific action that will get the ball rolling toward the solution you describe in paragraph 2.

• A RECIPE FOR THE ADJUSTMENT LETTER •

Paragraph 1:   Repeat the essence of the claim to which you are responding. This guarantees that there will be no miscommunication about the facts at hand.

Paragraph 2:   If you are granting a claim, say so. If you are not granting a claim, consider a "buffer" that eases into the negative message. Such buffers can include explanations, background information, or your expression of sympathy for the problem at hand.

Paragraph 3: Give any additional information necessary to your decision in paragraph 2. You may want to describe certain conditions, for example, or limitations.

Paragraph 4: Build goodwill by an expression of fellow-feeling. If appropriate, thank your reader for patience and understanding.

• A RECIPE FOR A COLLECTION LETTER •

The following recipe is appropriate for most earnest collection letters written *after* the "Have you forgotten?" note at the beginning of the collection process.

Paragraph 1: State what is owed, how long it has been overdue, and from what transaction.

Paragraph 2: State the urgency of the situation, perhaps with suggestions of what you will be forced to do if payment is not received.

Paragraph 3: Urge the reader to mail payment (repeat amount) by a specified date. Make sure that all address and account information necessary for the payment is included in your letter.

Minute  49

Presenting Documents

Too often we feel the business document is "done" when it returns in attractive form from word processing. It can then be shunted on its way to its intended audience.

How unfortunate. The act of presenting a document can be just as vital to its persuasive effect as the words it contains. Consider each of the following strategies when you send off business messages:

1. **Personal presentation.** Will the document be received in a more positive way if you deliver it by hand? Will you be able to answer quick questions on the spot that otherwise might trouble your reader? Will your reader sense the importance of the document as it arrives from your hand?

2. **Special mail presentation.** Should your message arrive along with all the other daily mail? Can it be distinguished by special postage—certified or registered, for example—or by special instructions on the envelope ("Confidential," "Time-dated materials," and so forth)?

3. **Special accompaniments.** Should your message arrive alone? Would it have more impact if it came with a sample, catalog, gift, or other accompaniment?

4. **Third parties.** Can someone else be useful to the persuasive effect of your document? Do you and your reader share a mutual friend or business acquaintance who might deliver your document to good effect?

Editing for Others

Perhaps because teachers have been so free in their criticism of our writing, we naturally tend to hide it from one another in the workplace. Even though two midlevel managers can kibbitz freely about improving their golf swings, they can't break free to discuss improving their writing.

Push, however, soon comes to shove. You find yourself in a managerial role where you *must* edit the work coming out of your unit before it sees the light of day. As a crash course in the delicate art of editing someone else's writing, consider the ten commandments of editing:

1. **Thou shalt explain.** Let your writers know why you're making changes. Otherwise, they will resent your interference as "high-handed" and, more important, never change their writing behavior (or misbehavior). Your explanations don't have to be couched in formal grammatical terms. Just explain in a commonsense way ("I'm using shorter words to make more impact.") what you are doing and why.
2. **Thou shalt clarify.** Never let writing pass on the grounds that "Well, I don't understand it, but others probably will." You are the judge and jury deciding the clarity of the writing at hand.
3. **Thou shalt shorten and simplify.** Most writing in business is *over*writing. Show your writers how to have their say in a few words.
4. **Thou shalt not be sarcastic.** Never use a broad, biting comment ("Such a flair for style, Frank!") as an editing

technique. Struggling writers need your specific suggestions for improvement, not blame.

5. **Thou shalt not compare.** It does little good as an office editor to set up a pecking order (even a hunt-and-peck order) among your writers. Telling Sally that she should write more like Gloria won't help either writer or office relations. Define what you like about Gloria's style, and then discuss those qualities—sans the reference to Gloria—with Sally.

6. **Thou shalt be patient.** Good business writing does not happen overnight. Your work in building the skills of your writers may take months. The effort and patience is worth the reward, both for the company and the people involved.

7. **Thou shalt read carefully.** Careful editing demands your close attention to what the writer is trying to say. Don't imitate the practice of one manager/editor who simply circled all occurrences of "is" in a wrong-headed effort to encourage active verbs. Instead, try to understand the essence of the writer's message. Then begin to evaluate the words used to convey that message.

8. **Thou shalt not do it thyself.** Especially during hassled business days, many editors—for expedience, they say—simply take over writing and rewriting chores themselves. They take pride in being able to write quickly and well. Don't do it. Struggling writers must stay in the battle if they are ever to win.

9. **Thou shalt pass out more praise than blame.** Writers are used to criticism: they have received it in full measure for most of the writing they have done from their earliest years. Remember that learners respond to praise more than to blame. Find some aspect of business documents to praise: "This opening is great, Bill."

10. **Thou shalt set a good example.** Practice what you preach around the office by taking care—even in incidental memos—to demonstrate the power and effectiveness of clear, crisp writing.

Saying No

We all say "yes" in writing more easily than "no." "Yes" leaves us smelling like a rose, in favor with the whole world. "No" disappoints our reader at best and gives us a new enemy at worst.

Saying "no" effectively and politely is a crucial business skill. Most managers report saying "no" much more frequently than "yes"—"no" to vacation requests, raises, proposals, and so forth. Managers who say "yes" too frequently, in fact, often find themselves overcommitted and their companies financially imperiled.

Learn to say "no" by understanding what you are and are not saying. "No" does not mean "I don't like you." "No" does not mean you're shutting the last door to the happiness of the requestor. Actually, much of our anxiety over saying "no" stems directly from egotism: we can't imagine how the requestor can go on living and breathing after we've said "no."

Come off it. In the same way that the requestor gets up the nerve to ask, you can get up the nerve to say "no." You can say it with understanding, even empathy, in your eyes and expression. But you don't have to feel guilty over your negative answer—any more than the requestor has to feel guilty for asking.

Should you explain your "no" answer? Whenever possible and appropriate, yes. We like to think that we live in a rational world when "no" can be justified for good reasons. By explaining your thinking, you are reassuring your requestor that your answer isn't based on personal disliking.

At times, however, extended explanations cause more problems than they solve. Explaining *why* you can't grant credit to an applicant, for example, may involve you in a long, expensive, and legally hazardous written rehearsal of his or her credit history.

In such cases, say "no" politely and move directly to possible alternatives. In most cases, your reader will not care about the absence of an explanation so long as a ready alternative exists.

And what about situations where no alternatives exist? Again, don't feel guilty. A request does not create the obligation on your part to provide viable alternatives. A request for a loan, for example, must often be met with a simple, direct "no": "We cannot approve your request for a loan at this time." Much better at such moments to make a simple statement of "no" than to set the requestor off on a wild goose-chase of questionable alternatives.

Managers who say "no" reasonably and politely soon learn that they make more real friends than they lose. Fair, insightful decision-makers attract the respect of others by their skill in communicating negative answers without arousing hostility or feeling guilt.

Minute  52

Reading for Improvement

How can you continue to improve your business writing? We would like to think that this book gives you lessons a-plenty for the short term. But after mastering these techniques, you can build and refine your skills by *reading good writing*.

We learn to write by reading. Our inner "ear" captures the flow of what we read; we pour out those rhythms and phrases in the sentences we write.

But how can you cultivate that all-important inner ear for language?

Read good stuff. Novels will do quite well—and not necessarily "heavy" novels studied in universities. Most best sellers have passed the scrupulous review of professional editors and, no matter what the content, have many stylistic virtues. So read your favorite works with gusto, even reading aloud at times to hear how words rise and fall, surge and subside. Listen for how the writer emphasizes key words and varies sentence types. Notice how the writer keeps you from boredom.

If you're not a novel reader, turn to good business writing—the kind found in *Fortune, Forbes, Business Week, Harvard Business Review, The Wall Street Journal*, and other major publications. Again, read for style as well as for content. Notice sentence length. Read aloud to hear—and thereby capture for your own use—the rhythms of professional style.

These activities will serve you well over a career in advancing not only the quality of your own style but also the speed with which you can pour your thoughts onto paper.

Minute

53

Creating Resumes

Consider the following 20 pieces of advice when creating or evaluating your own resume:

1. Make your name stand out. You want to be remembered.
2. During business hours, who will answer the telephone at the number you list on your resume? If the answer is "no one," buy an answer machine.
3. In listing a career goal, be careful not to sound unambitious or overly ambitious. While you may want to be CEO of a major corporation at some future date, set a more immediate and attainable goal for most applications.
4. Decide whether your education or experience is most impressive. If education portrays you best, put it first on your resume. Otherwise, let experience take the first position.
5. Don't go back to high school in describing your education unless you have no college experience or you have regional/national honors (such as National Merit Scholarships, etc.) from high school.
6. Do list your GPA if it was B or better. Remember that you can choose between your cumulative GPA or GPA in your major, depending on which was higher. Identify the GPA you choose.
7. Courses often have impressive titles ("Macroeconomics") and can be placed in the education section to good effect. Don't list more than five or six key courses.
8. Employers are often interested in your future educational plans. If you plan to undertake graduate study, for example, say so. You may, however, want to reassure your em-

ployer that such study won't mean you'll be quitting your job.

9. In turning to the experience portion of your resume, decide whether your job title ("Assistant Manager") or the company (IBM) is most impressive. List in order of prestige value.

10. List experience from most recent to least recent. You don't have to account for each month of your work history. Select employment that represents you well.

11. Be sure to list responsibilities for each position you've held. These can be stated as brief phrases (". . . handled cash disbursements") and probably won't number more than three or four.

12. Place the dates (month and year is sufficient) of your employment after the job title and company. The reader should not be tempted to concentrate on dates instead of what you did.

13. The personal background section of your resume should portray you as a healthy, active, involved person. If travel will be important to your application, suggest that you like to travel and are free to do so. Age and sex need not be mentioned unless they bear upon your chances for the job. Similarly, you can choose to discuss your marital status and any children if you feel your application will be stronger for doing so.

14. Whenever possible, include three references (name, title, address, and phone) on the resume itself. Often these references will not be contacted, but their impressive names and titles will do you good as the reader glances over the resume. (This advice is somewhat controversial: some authorities recommend that references *not* be placed on the resume.)

15. Remember that resumes should "deliver the goods" within 20 or 30 seconds. Especially when working through a stack of applicants, employers make screening decisions based on very quick impressions of your resume. Emphasize key points, arrange your words attractively, and keep it brief. Resumes exceed one or two pages only at their peril.

16. Unless you have good reason for doing so, omit your picture from your resume. Most employers prefer not to have

knowledge of such matters as your race when making hiring decisions.

17. If you can afford the modest expense, have your resume typeset on heavy bond stationery. Prefer conservative white or buff paper to pastels.

18. Accompany each resume you send with an application letter that mentions the job for which you're applying, a highlight or two from your resume, and your earnest wish for an interview.

19. Carry extra resumes with you to interviews. Your original submission may have been lost or other interviewers may need a copy.

20. Above all, remember that your resume is not yours at all. In every way, it is aimed at "them"—what they need to know about you to make a favorable decision. Before placing any item of information on the resume, therefore, evaluate it from the readers' point of view. What will it contribute to their favorable impression of you?

Minute  54

Writing for the Senses

Suppose you're done with your document. Before giving yourself a well-deserved pat on the back ask yourself, "Have I applied the message to the reader?" To find out, strip away grammar, style, logic, and document choice. What else is there? *The senses.*

Writing for the senses means fitting new information into a structure the reader already knows. By doing so, you create a scene and place the reader there. For instance, consider the following passage:

> The steps are really quite easy. First, take the items and organize them. How you separate the piles is really up to you. But whatever you do, be consistent. Next, put the items in their respective slots, set up storage, and place them accordingly.

Get the picture? It's doubtful that anyone would. Now let's take a look at the same passage revised for the reader:

> Filing documents is really quite simple. First, group the documents by customer or type, but not both. Next, place the documents in manila folders, write a name or code on each, and place them alphabetically in the file cabinet.

Readers would be hard pressed to remember the details of the first passage. Yet the second passage would be easy for anyone to remember. That's because it puts the procedure in context, thereby placing the reader in the scene. The reader can then draw inferences and organize the material accordingly.

So how do you know what the reader thinks? It's best to use your intuition and try to take the reader's point of view. Take into account background, education, lifestyle, environment, and business. Then use words of the senses—concrete, specific, primary words.

Primary words are words we all know. Secondary words must be translated using primary words. The following examples show the differences between primary and secondary words:

Primary	*Secondary*
Trustee	Fiduciary
Name	Nomenclature
Obstacle	Impediment
Take	Confiscate
Confuse	Obfuscate
Insist	Stipulate
Steal	Pilfer
Reject	Repudiate
Slander	Denigrate
Compliant	Obsequious
Unaware	Oblivious
Kind	Beneficent

Remember, writing for the senses means being sensitive to your reader's needs. If you apply this humanistic skill, then your words will conjure up the appropriate business images for your reader.

Minute  55

Getting Feedback

Feedback measures the effectiveness of your message—whether or not it "gets through" to the reader. To get feedback, you must first seek it.

Prior Feedback

Of course, most of us get feedback prior to sending the document to the intended reader. We ask a friend or officemate, "How does it read?" or "Is it clear?" And more often than not, we get these kinds of responses:

- "Not *our* style."
- "Doesn't quite get to the point."
- "Too imaginative—they'll never buy it."
- "Too, uh . . . I can't quite put my finger on it."
- "Too radical."

You have to be on guard when asking for advice from self-made editors. Their intentions are good, but they speak in generalities. It's best then, to ask someone whose judgment you trust—someone who will give you *specific suggestions*.

Two other pointers: Look at your trusted reader's eyes. What do they say? Next, don't take it personally, or you may never get advice again.

Feedback from the Recipient

The most important feedback comes from your *intended readers*. But first you have to decide how to get it. Will it be by phone, by questionnaire, reader inquiry card, etc.? You must provide the means for feedback.

Of course the mechanism for feedback depends on your objective and, thus, on which document you choose. The chart below suggests different forms of feedback by document type.

Document	Objective	Reader Feedback
Memo	Gain approval for suggested actions	Check box Initial line
Letter	Obtain response to request	Phone number Follow-up call
Proposal	Motivate to adopt proposed actions	Contract Phone number
Report	Get response and motivate to act on recommendations	Phone number Response page
Questionnaire	Get response to questionnaire	Tear-away folded form Postage paid
Ad	Obtain sales leads Motivate buyers	Reader inquiry cards Postage paid
Direct mail	Obtain sales leads Motivate buyers	Responsorial card Postage paid

Playing Devil's Advocate

Your writing seems flawless, but a potential client rejects your proposal or the boss scuttles your report and says, "Do it over again." What happened? Chances are you forgot to think of alternative viewpoints.

Whenever you write, apply the words to the situation. Take different points of view; play devil's advocate. Though it may not be fun to bare the "soul" of your words to "sinful" criticism, it's a necessary evil. So here are a few ways to play the game of devil's advocate:

1. **Viewing the spectrum.** Take the major points of your document. For each point, take one or two decidedly different viewpoints. Now criticize the point from each perspective. Does your argument hold up? If not, perhaps you need to rethink the document.

2. **Taking the vote.** Ask three different people to vote on your letter, proposal, or report. Don't give any explanations. Just ask them to vote yes or no to this question: Do you buy it?

3. **Pinning the tail on the donkey.** Play pin the tail on the donkey. In other words, try to IDENTIFY any kind of *problem* (argument, packaging, tone, document choice, length, approach, etc.) with the document. Once you've pinned the tail on the donkey, try to buck it off the page!

4. **Putting your money where your mouth is.** Let's say your document proposes an action or makes recommendations. Make believe that your money is at stake. Would you accept the proposal, report, or letter?

5. **Turning a new leaf.** Just to dust the cobwebs out, write the letter, proposal, or report in a different way. Try to mold the business document to the content rather than using a stock form.

Writing for Electronic Mail

Electronic mail (sending messages directly from computer terminal to computer terminal via electronic mailboxes) is here to stay. Better, it's here to replace many of our traditional ways of delivering paper messages.

Let's assume, in fact, that by 1995 most messages in businesses will be sent, received, and stored electronically. So what?

For writers, the answer to that question lies in changing some aspects of their most basic writing habits. Just as our speaking changed in subtle and not-so-subtle ways when we turned to using the telephone, so our writing will change to meet the limitations and possibilities of electronic mail. Consider four changes you may want to make as you adapt to electronic mail:

1. Practice "early messaging," placing your main communication at the beginning of electronic messages. (Reading from the computer screen is more difficult than from paper—readers will want to grasp your message as quickly as possible.)
2. Reduce the number of words in your message. Electronic mail messages *look* and *feel* twice as long as the same number of words on paper.
3. Personalize your message, using all the "warmth" techniques described in earlier lessons. You can't count on a classy letterhead, heavy bond stationery, or a swirling signature to influence your reader in electronic mail. You must rely only on your ability to convey your thoughts and personality by words.

4. Don't rely on elaborate formats such as double or triple interior margins to communicate the organizational scheme of your communication. Such formats often aren't possible within the limits of the electronic mail system you may be using.

Minute  58

Writing with a Word Processor

Users of word processors report a "conversion experience" of sorts. They have forgiven their fingers, those culprits that previously used to mess up important documents. For example, a sentence mistyped on a traditional typewriter usually entailed the retyping of the entire page.

But using word processing, the forgiven fingers know they can do no irretrievable harm. Consequently, they relax. They type faster (20 to 30 percent faster) than they did before.

Better, they let you compose on the screen. You no longer have to draft documents by hand in preparation for chiseling them into the granite of type. Now words can be canceled, corrected, rearranged, and printed out with ease.

The message for the writer is simple: get onto a word processor as quickly as possible. Your production speed will probably double within the first six months. The quality of your work will increase as well. Studies have shown that users of word processors edit three or more times as much as traditional typists, due largely to the fact that editing is so easy on the screen.

Writing as a Team

Camels must tire of the old joke: they are really horses designed by a committee. And writers, too, are usually sick and tired of trying to write by committee. We've all been there: the endless discussions, the starts and stops, the bruised egos and misunderstandings. Often one writer in the group simply volunteers to "do the damn thing," then to pass it around for improvement by others.

Such problems can be avoided. Teams can write effectively, and often must on larger projects. Here are five suggestions for turning chaos into concert:

1. Agree on strict time limits. "Let's spend no more than 15 minutes brainstorming. After that, we'll divide up the work among the group." Such time limits force everyone to have their say in a succinct way—and give hope to the group that something (hopefully progress) will take place at the end of the time limit.

2. Divide up writing tasks with the mutual agreement that *everyone* has to *produce* for the next meeting of the team. Absolutely no excuses will be accepted. This peer pressure will help each member break writer's block. It's always too easy to make up excuses for why a document can't be written.

3. Develop a team spirit of optimism and support. When someone presents a draft of their portion of the project, find something to praise before turning to criticism. In this way, team members will gain confidence and, with it, speed in writing and thinking.

4. Settle upon general models for development, the "flow" of the document. How should pages "look"? How should major points be supported? What use should be made of graphics?
5. Resolve stylistic differences at the *end* of the writing project, not in midstream. Writers need their own voices during the drafting period of the project. Don't stifle them by insisting on a particular style.

Checking Your Work

When all is said and done, five things matter most of all in written documents. Use this checklist to evaluate your own documents and those written by others:

1. Should the document be more clear?
2. Should the document be better organized?
3. Should the document be more attractive?
4. Should the document emphasize its key points more forcefully?
5. Should the document be shorter or longer?

Part Five

Writer's Toolbox: A Basic Resource for Business Writers

• COMMAS •

The comma sections off *nonessential* parts of the sentence. Without these sections the sentence could still function as a complete sentence. Let's take a look at when to use the comma:

1. Between independent clauses (both clauses contain a subject and a verb) joined by and, but, and for:

   Kantron Company decided to expand into the industrial market, but it decided to hold off on the government market.

2. After any introductory phrase:

   Using satellite transmission, computers send messages around the globe in seconds.

3. To separate words in a series:

   The company has decided to use gray, maroon, green, and blue on its corporate logo.

Many examples abound, but the point is that commas serve to separate different bits of information or nonessentials. In example 3, the colors had to be separated by commas. Otherwise we wouldn't know if the last color was "blue" or "green and blue." Three more examples of when to use a comma follow:

4. To separate parenthetical expressions from the rest of the sentence:

   The president nominated the judge, who had been a former Arizona state senator, to the Supreme Court Bench.

5. Before and after year dates when the month dates come before:

   On July 4, 1986, the new toy company will introduce its robot line.

6. Before and after a state name when the city comes before:

   Del Mar Motors chose Chicago, Illinois, as the site of its new auto plant.

• SEMICOLONS •

Semicolons are long, heavy commas that separate two units, sentences. To accomplish this, the semicolon combines the comma and the period. The comma part of the semicolon indicates that the two sentences should be considered separate parts of a whole unit of thought. The period part of the semicolon indicates that the two units are, indeed, sentences. So, the semicolon gives the sentences both closure (the period) and relation (the comma).

The semicolon can be used in a variety of instances. The first word of the sentence following should not be capitalized. The three most common semicolon uses follow. Use a semicolon:

1. To relate sentences when a conjunction (and, but, for) is omitted.

   Winter sales for Alpine Ski Company are usually high; summer sales are typically low.

2. Before conjunctive adverbs (therefore) or illustrative phrases (for instance).

   The production of delicate telescopic prisms is ahead of schedule; therefore, we can make six extra units.

3. In a series that contain commas.

   Many Southern California companies have increased their research and development costs: Kantron, 30 percent; Cabbot, 20 percent; and Matrix, 15 percent.

• COLONS •

Except when used in salutations (Dear Mr. Appleton:), ad signs (For Rent: 40 Offices), and time figures (2:15 P.M.), the colon follows a complete sentence. A list of words, phrases, and even sentences can follow the colon. Usually, business writers use the colon in three situations. Use a colon:

1. To suggest a list will follow a complete sentence.

   Kantron, Inc., decided to develop artificial eyes for three reasons: new lens were available, research money was plentiful, and glaucoma was increasing.

2. To stress an appositive (noun used to explain a preceding noun).

   The company was concerned with one thing: quality. (Not only a colon, but also a dash or a comma would be acceptable punctuation in example 2.)

3. To indicate that a formal statement follows.

Each Hanover representative must ask himself or herself this question: Do my values fit in with company goals?

Common Errors

1. Using a colon after a preposition (to) or a transitive verb (verb such as "include" that requires something to follow).
2. Using a colon after one word in a business memo.

   Use: 1. Sales Log Sheet.
            2. Engineering Work Order.
            3. Regional Reference Number.

Instead, write "Use the following items:"

• DASHES •

Dashes "—" are informal connectors. When two words are somehow related we use a hyphen "-", but when two thoughts or ideas are related we use a dash. Dashes can be used in the following instances:

1. To place emphasis on appositives.

The company was concerned with one thing—quality.
The storm—the severest in years—delayed all flights.
(A colon or comma could be used in the first instance.)

2. When appositives contain commas.

The three employees with the highest productivity rates—Jackie, 3.07; Ed, 3.10; and Debra, 3.23—were honored at the company awards ceremony.

3. When parenthetical remarks contain changes in thought.

The Grace Commission reported—though the report was condemned by some congressmen—that the government has overlapping services, inefficient purchasing procedures, and incompatible computer systems.

• PARENTHESES •

Parentheses indicate afterthoughts and provide explanatory material. They should be used when the parenthetical material would otherwise interfere with the rest of the sentence. Parentheses should be used in the following instances:

1. For explanatory material and examples that could be omitted.

   Our first office to open in New York (on 5th Avenue) has performed beyond our highest profit projections.

2. To provide a check when writing figures.

   This advanced security system sells for fifty-three thousand dollars ($53,000).

3. After a period when the whole sentence is parenthetical; before a period when the last part is parenthetical.

   The company claimed three extraordinary losses. (They had not reported any in the past decade.)

   Chrysler's rejuvenation was engineered by one man, Lee Iacocca (a registered Democrat).

• PUNCTUATION RECAP: COMMAS, SEMICOLONS, COLONS, DASH, PARENTHESES •

Using these few toolbox rules, you should be able to punctuate your sentences with confidence. Of course, as business writers, it's convenient to have a handy source around. So rather than rereading commas, semicolons, colons, dashes, and parentheses—the *sentence separators*—the following chart summarizes *when* to use them:

	Before Appositives	End of a Sentence	Separate Series	Before Lists	Separate Nonessentials
,	Yes	No	Yes	No	Yes
;	No	Yes	Yes*	No	No
:	Yes†	Yes	No	Yes	No
—	Yes	No	No	No	Yes
( )	Yes	Some	No	No	Yes

*Before appositives occurring at the end of a sentence.
†When items in a series contain commas.

• QUOTATION MARKS •

Use quotations marks for

1. Direct quotations.

   The company president remarked, "Increased growth means increased opportunities."

2. Titles of short works.

   Article: "The Coming of Age of the MOS Chip Camera."
   Chapter: "Advances in Hydroponics."
   Song: "As Time Goes By."

Position quotation marks as follows:

1. Periods and commas go inside end quotes.

   "Don't just stand there," bellowed the manager, "We've got a business to run."

2. Colons and semicolons go outside quotation marks.

   Ted ordered, "We'll each have the frank and bean special"; however, Lola interrupted saying, "I'd rather have the lobster."

3. Question marks and exclamation marks go inside quotation marks only if they are part of the quotation.

   Mr. Finch said, "Are there any questions?"
   Why did she say, "Next week is the deadline"?

• ITALICS •

Italics was first used in an Italian edition of Virgil's works, printed in Venice in 1501. Today, business writers use italics for emphasis. Since most typewriters and some printers do not have special characters for italic print, writers typically underline text to indicate italics. Use italics for

1. Emphasis.

   The meeting has been changed to *Wednesday* noon instead of *Friday* noon.

2. Foreign words and phrases.

The priest still signs his letters with *Dominus vobiscum,* or the "Lord be with you."

3. Titles of major works.

Gone with the Wind depicts an era that truly is gone with the wind.

• APOSTROPHES •

Most of us trip over apostrophes, but it's really just a matter of forming (1) possessives, (2) contractions, and (3) special plurals.

Possessives

As you write, think *who owns what.* You indicate this ownership by forming the possessive. In many cases, you can substitute the phrase "belongs to" to see if the possessive is necessary. Possessives come in two flavors: singular and plural.

Singular Possessive.   Form the singular possessive like this: Singular noun + " 's".

The accountant's books indicated an error. (Ask yourself, do the books belong to the accountant? The answer is yes. Hence the singular possessive.)

Singular nouns ending in "s" usually require an " 's".

Ms. Wyss's report was well received. (Exception: Words two syllables or more ending in "s" require only an apostrophe. Example: Moses' laws.)

Plural Possessive.   Form the plural possessive like this: Plural noun + Apostrophe.

The representatives' offer was accepted. (Exception: Plural noun not ending in "s" forms the possessive by adding " 's". Example: Women's rights.)

When to Use Possessives.   You have two kinds of possessives to use: singular and plural. So when should you use them? Use possessives to

1. Show ownership.

   The boss's files were missing.
   Mr. Tanaka's statement was informative.
   The boys' cousins wanted their own bicycles.

2. Show time or distance in the possessive.

   We embarked on a long winter's journey.
   Last month's profit reports showed a downturn in sales.
   (Apostrophe substitutes for the preposition. Otherwise, you'd write "The profit reports of last month . . .)

3. Precede a gerund (verbal phrase).

   Ms. O'Reilly's pounding the gavel proved her insistence on order in the court.

Common Errors.   These two are the main culprits:

1. Possessive pronouns such as their, theirs, your, yours, our, ours, her, hers, it, and its do not take an apostrophe. ("It's" is the contraction for "it is.")

2. Whether to use a singular or plural possessive depends on the possessive noun, NOT the noun being possessed. Example: The manager's report, the managers' reports.

Contractions

Apostrophes mark where one or more letters have been omitted in contractions. Note that contractions make writing seem less formal.

I'm = I am	wouldn't = would not
she'd = she would	didn't = did not
you're = you are	it's = it is
they've = they have	

Special Plurals

Use apostrophes to form the plurals of abbreviations, letters, acronyms, symbols, and figures. (Note that the trend is to omit the apostrophe unless it would be confusing.)

Ph.D's   W's   BMW's   +'s   1980's

• CAPITALIZATION •

In effect, capitals say to the reader "me first," because they make words stand out in a crowd. Most of us shudder at the thought of trying to understand the complex web of exceptions in capitalization. It's best not to try to memorize all of the exceptions but to memorize a few general rules. Capitalize the following:

1. First words of sentences and direct quotations.

    In today's world, no man is an island.

    He said, "Profits rose last quarter."

2. Proper nouns.

    Names of—
        a. Persons and titles preceding names:
            Professor Adams   General Patton
            Uncle Louie
            But: my professor   that general   her uncle
        b. Specific places and regions:
            Rhode Island   Lake Erie   Los Angeles
            the North
            But: an island   a lake   a city   to fly north
        c. Organizations and their members:
            Catholics   California Museum of Science and Industry
        d. Ships, planes, and spacecraft:
            Queen Mary   *Concorde*   *Apollo V*
        e. Groups, races, and nationalities:
            Caucasian   Negro   Hispanic   Danish
            German
        f. Days, months, holidays:
            Monday   July   Christmas
        g. Historical periods and events:
            World War I   Industrial Age

3. Artistic works.

    Books: James A. Michener's *Space.*
              Sidney Sheldon's *If Tomorrow Comes.*
    Poems: Emily Dickinson's "The Secret."

Songs: Simon & Garfunkle's "Bridge over Troubled
          Water."
Symphonies: *Pastoral Symphony*
Screenplays: *Back to the Future*

• MISPLACED MODIFIERS •

General Rule

A modifier, a phrase that describes or alters the meaning of another word, must be placed next to that word in the sentence. Here are a few examples showing what happens when modifiers are misplaced. Each sentence below can be corrected by placing the group of words in brackets next to the italicized word.

1. In accordance with your *instructions,* I have developed two new machines [in the enclosed envelope].
2. [At a historic high], the Federal Reserve chairman defended the prime lending *rate.*
3. At the department luncheon, we served *platters* to our employees [with spaghetti on them].
4. Iris, the orbiting telescope, will send an infrared *photo* back to earth [which shows planetary rings].

• PRONOUNS •

Why is the pronoun the nostalgic noun? Because it *looks back* to find its antecedent (noun it refers to). The word *pro* literally means "before in place or position." Thus, the pronoun almost always refers to a noun or pronoun nearest to it.

The general rule for pronoun choice goes like this: Pronouns must agree with their antecedents in number and gender. Now, let's take a look at seven basic applications of this rule:

1. **Singular antecedents.**

    The *businessman* has *his* own computer.

2. **Plural antecedents.**

    The *researchers* have *their* own offices.

3. **Compound antecedents.**

   My *boss* and my *boss's boss* got *their* raises.

4. **Indefinite pronoun antecedents.**

   Each of the foremen has *his* own car.

5. **Subjective case.**

   I, we, you, he, she, it, and they all function as subjects.

   My co-worker and *I* left work early.

   Peter's most productive workers are Jeanine and *he*.

6. **Objective case.**

   Me, us, you, him, her, it, and them function as direct or indirect objects or objects of prepositions.

   The construction worker called John and *us* over.

   The clothing store refunded *me* the money.

7. **Who or whom.**

   Who is a subject, and whom is an object. Or another way to look at it is "Who gives, and Whom receives."

   I gave my report to my assistant *who* distributed it to the department. (Who is the subject of "distributed.")

   The consultant *whom* I have dealt with before is John. (Turn the phrase around to "I have dealt with whom.")

• AGREEMENT •

General Rule

Verbs must agree with their subject in number.

1. Singular subjects take singular verbs.

   The *manager talks* to her employees.

   The engineering *meeting is* ready to begin.

   There *was* just one *speaker* at the conference.

2. Plural and compound subjects take plural verbs.

   Both *management* and the *union were* satisfied with the agreement (compound).

   Both floor *supervisors play* golf together every Saturday (plural).

3. Indefinite pronouns come in two varieties: (*a*) singular and (*b*) singular or plural.

    a. The following indefinite pronouns take singular verbs: each, either, neither, one, everyone, everybody, no one, nobody, anyone, anybody, someone, and somebody.

    Each of the employees *has* a recommendation.

    b. Depending on the context of the sentence, the following indefinite pronouns can take either singular or plural verb forms: all, any, none, some, more, most.

    Most of the billing *is* finished.

    Most of the bills of lading *are* prepared.

• SPELLING •

Ever get stung by the spelling bee? Like the bear that sticks a paw in the hornets nest thinking it's a honey jar, we've all been stung before. Let's face it, spelling can be a very sticky business.

George Bernard Shaw observed that "fish" could be spelled "ghoti" using the "f" sound from "enough," the "i" sound from "women," and the "sh" sound from "fiction." In fact the "sh" sound can be written at least 12 ways:

creation	oceanography
pshaw	sugarplum
chivalry	issuant
concession	coercion
shop	gaseous
fuchsia	conscience

Rules

So much for the eccentricities (or is that eggcentricities?) of spelling. The good news is that there are methods to the madness. Here are THE 12 KEYS TO BETTER SPELLING:

Key 1: For one syllable words ending in consonant-vowel-consonant, double the final consonant before adding a suffix beginning with a vowel.

Word	+	*Suffix*	=	*New word*
ship		er		shipper
flag		ed		flagged
tag		ing		tagging
ton		age		tonnage
big		est		biggest

Key 2: For words ending in "E" preceded by a consonant, omit the "E" before adding a suffix that begins with a vowel.

Word	+	*Suffix*	=	*New word*
slope		ing		sloping
desire		able		desirable
please		antry		pleasantry
observe		ation		observation
telephone		ing		telephoning

Key 3: For two-syllable words ending in consonant-vowel-consonant and accented on the second syllable, double the final consonant before adding a suffix that begins with a vowel.

Word	+	*Suffix*	=	*New word*
transfer		ing		transferring
confer		ed		conferred
transmit		er		transmitter
incur		ence		incurrence
infer		ed		inferred

Key 4: Except in "science," "I" before "E" except after "C."

receive   conceive

perceive

Key 5: When adding prefixes to roots, do not omit letters.

mis + spell = misspell
over + rule = overrule
room + mate = roommate

Key 6: Six words end in "ery"; the rest end in "ary."

millinery	monastery
confectionery	cemetery
stationery	distillery
(paper)	

Key 7: Only four words end in "efy"; the rest end in "ify."

stupefy	putrefy
liquefy	rarefy

Key 8: For words ending in "e," drop the "e" before adding "able." If a word ends in two "e's," keep them.

admirable
lovable
agreeable

Key 9: Add "able" if the base is a full word, but add "ible" if it's not.

credible	reprehensible
responsible	incredible
permissible	

Key 10: Make a mark beside every word you look up in the dictionary. Learn the meaning and spelling of a new word every time you open the dictionary.

Key 11: Learn how to pronounce words in order to spell them.

Key 12: Learn this list of 140 most commonly misspelled words:

absence	affect (verb)	asterisk
acceptance	all right	athletics
accessible	a lot	auxiliary
achieve	altogether	awhile (adverb)
acquaint	all together	awkward
adjustable	analyze	bachelor
advantageous	anonymous	beginning
advertising	assistance	believable

• MOST COMMONLY MISSPELLED WORDS •

belligerent	embarrassing	personnel
benefited	exaggerate	possesses
boundary	exceed	precede
bureaucratic	extraordinary	predictable
calendar	fallacy	preferred
campaign	flexible	privilege
canceled	grammar	procedure
cannot	hypocrisy	proceed
category	illegible	pronunciation
changeable	independent	psychology
clientele	insistent	questionnaire
column	intermediary	receive
collateral	irresistible	recommend
committee	judgment	repetition
comparable	judicial	rescind
compelled	kindergarten	rhythmical
competitor	legitimate	sacrilegious
compliment	loose	salable
complement	maintenance	secretary
conceive	mathematics	seize
conferred	mediocre	separate
conscience	minimum	sergeant
continuing	misspelling	stationary
controlled	necessary	stationery
convenient	negligence	succeed
correspondence	negotiable	suddenness
council	newsstand	superintendent
counsel	nickel	supersede
credibility	noticeable	surgeon
criterion	occurrence	surprise
criteria	organize	tangible
criticism	opponent	technique
defendent	pamphlet	tenant
definitely	parallel	tyrannize
desirable	pastime	unanimous
disappear	peaceable	vacillate
disappoint	penicillin	wholly
dissatisfied	permanent	yield
eligible	persistent	

• PLURALS •

Variety is the spice of life. So too with the English language. Take noun forms. Most plurals are formed by adding an "s" or an "es" to the end of a noun. Yet a few lovable mutants keep most of us grasping for the dictionary. The following chart provides a guide for forming unusual plurals:

Classification	Singular	Plural	Rule
Nouns ending in:			
y preceded by vowel	attorney	attorneys	Add "s"
preceded by consonant	company	companies	Omit "y" Add "ies"
f	handkerchief	handkerchiefs	Some nouns add "s"
	half	halves	Some add "yes"
fe	safe	safes	Some add "yes"
	life	lives	
o preceded by vowel	portfolio	portfolios	Add "s"
preceded by consonant	tuxedo	tuxedos	Some nouns add "s"
musical term	veto	vetoes	Some add "es"
two plurals	alto	altos	Add "s"
	cargo	cargos cargoes	
	mosquito	mosquitos mosquitoes	
	memento	memento mementoes	
Compound nouns:			
Hyphenated with noun	mother-in-law	mothers-in-law	Principle noun pluralized
Hyphenated without noun	wrap-up	wrap-ups	Final word pluralized
Not hyphenated	business-woman	business-women	Final word pluralized
Plural nouns:		scissors pliers thanks	Always plural
Singular nouns:	news physics linguistics		Always singular

Classification	Singular	Plural	Rule
People:			*Replace with*
	man	*men*	*"a"* *"e"*
	woman	*women*	
	child	*children*	*(Add "ren")*
Anatomy:	foot	feet	"oo" "ee"
	tooth	teeth	
Animals:	goose	geese	"oo" "ee"
	mouse	mice	"ous" "ic"
	ox	oxen	(Add "en")
	moose	moose	
	sheep	sheep	
	deer	deer	
	octopus	octopi	"us" "i"

• OUR STRANGE LANGUAGE •

We'll begin with a box and the plural is boxes,
But the plural of ox is oxen, not oxes.
Then, one fowl is a goose but two are called geese,
Yet the plural of moose should never be meese.

You find a lone mouse or a whole set of mice,
Yet the plural of house is houses, not hice.
If the plural of man is always called men,
Why shouldn't the plural of pan be called pen?

If I speak of a foot and you show me your feet,
And I give you a boot, would a pair be called beet?
If one is a tooth and a whole set are teeth,
Why shouldn't the plural of booth be called beeth?

Then, one may be that, and three would be those,
Yet hat in the plural wouldn't be hose.
We speak of a brother and also say brethren,
But though we say Mother, we never say Methren.

Then, the masculine pronouns are he, his, and him,
But imagine the feminine she, shis, and shim.
So English, I fancy you all will agree,
Is the funniest language you ever did see.

Anonymous

• FREQUENTLY CONFUSED WORDS •

"You say accept, and I say except."
"You say affect, and I say effect."

"Accept, except; Affect, effect"
"Oh! Let's call the whole thing off."

Like Gershwin's song, we all confuse words from time to time; however, even if you're an expert, you must pay attention to usage, or readers may not pay attention to you. The following words are frequently confused:

1. **Accept, except.**

   Accept means to receive with consent or to give approval.
   Except means to exclude or to leave out a number or whole.

   I *accept* every point in your proposal *except* the last one on page two.

2. **Affect, effect.**

   Distinguish these two words by substituting their meanings in the sentence. For the verb *affect,* substitute "influence." For the verb *effect,* substitute "to bring about"; and for the noun *effect,* substitute "result."

   The company's reorganization should not *affect* your salary.

   Or: The company's reorganization should not *influence* your salary.

   The city council wants to *effect* a change in the current legislation.

   Or: The city council wants to *bring about* a change in the current legislation.

   The *effect* of the change will be known in July.

   Or: The *result* of the change will be known in July.

3. **All right** is all right, but **alright** is all wrong.

   The proposal figures were *all right.*
   That date is *all right* with me.

4. **All together, altogether.**

   All together means "in one group," but *altogether* means "entirely" or "completely."

   The managers were all together at the party.

   The group was altogether satisfied with the product.

5. **Among, between.**

   Two is *between,* three or more is *among.*

   The supply was split *among* the twelve people.

   The supply was split *between* the two people.

6. **Amount, number.**

   Amount should be used for money or things that cannot be counted. Use *number* for things that can be counted.

   The *amount* of work left on the project was enormous.

   The *number* of computers in our company has increased.

7. **Anxious, eager.**

   Eager should usually be used in business writing.

   Anxious should only be used when great concern or anxiety need to be expressed.

   The manager was eager to *accept* the company's offer.

   The woman was *anxious* about driving in the sleet.

8. **Complement, compliment.**

   Complement means to make complete or that which completes. *Compliment* means to praise.

   This product is a *complement* to the products you purchased earlier in the year.

   The employee was *complimented* for his outstanding performance.

9. **Continual, continuous.**

   A *continual* process may have planned breaks; a *continuous* one does not.

   The entrance is *continuously* being watched by the security camera. (The camera watches without breaks.)

   The washing machine has *continually* worked for the past four years. (It provided service over the past four year period, but it did not wash constantly.)

10. **Credible, creditable.**

    Credible means "believable"; *creditable* means "reputable."

    The statement the defendant made was *credible*.

    Mr. Stonewall's profitable investment decisions made him a *creditable* source of financial information.

11. **Disinterested, uninterested.**

    Disinterested means unbiased or free from selfish motive. The prefix *un* negates the base word so *uninterested* means not interested or not concerned.

    The two executives asked the advice of a *disinterested* manager to decide on the new medical plan.

    Since the engineer was extremely wealthy, he was *uninterested* in the cost of the Porsche.

12. **Each other, one another.**

    Each other refers to two people. *One another* refers to three or more people.

    The two businessmen help *each other* when ever possible.

    Our group was formed to help *one another* overcome writer's block.

13. **Eminent, imminent.**

    Eminent refers to something "well known," while *imminent* refers to something about to happen.

    The *eminent* writer will join our staff next week.

    The discovery of a cure for the common cold seems *imminent.*

14. **Farther, further.**

    Farther should be used when speaking in terms of distance. *Further* should be used when referring to extent or to degree.

    The store is much *farther* than two miles from your company.

    The strategy needs *further* clarification.

15. **Following, preceding.**

    Use *following* and *preceding* as adjectives, not nouns. Avoid "The following is" or "the preceding is."

The *following* actions should be taken soon.

The *preceding* announcement should be considered immediately.

16. **In, into.**

    In signifies a place; *into* signifies an action.

    The document is *in* the Mosler.

    She went *into* the office.

17. **Infer, imply.**

    Infer means to conclude. *Imply* means to suggest.

    I *infer* from your report that you find the system inadequate.

    Do you mean to *imply* that the system is inadequate?

18. **Its, it's.**

    It's is a contraction for it is. *Its* is a possessive pronoun.

    The candy has lost *its* flavor.

    It's a hectic schedule.

19. **Lie, lay.**

    Lie is a verb meaning to be at rest or inactive; whereas, *lay* is a verb meaning to place.

    Please *lie* down until you're feeling better.

    Please *lay* the information on my desk.

20. **Your, you're.**

    Your means "of or relating to you or yourselves" especially as possessor or possessors. *You're* is a contraction for "you are." To tell the difference substitute *you are* instead of *your* or *you're*.

    Is this *your* report?

    Not: Is this *you are* report?

    You're spending too much money.

    Or: *You are* spending too much money.

• STANDARD ABBREVIATIONS •

The following general rules are guidelines for when abbreviations are appropriate.

- Abbreviate months and days in charts and tables but not in standard text.

  The entire project is due in August 1986. (In this case, Aug 1986 or 10/86 is not appropriate.)

- Symbol forms of abbreviations may be used in visual aids but not in standard text.

  82.1 in. or 82.1 inches, not 82.1″

  62 percent, not 62%

- Abbreviate a unit of measurement only if it is used with a number.

  The paper should be cut in 4 in. squares.

  The length of the paper is measured in square inches.

- Eliminate periods in abbreviated forms of companies, private organizations, governmental agencies, and other groups.

ABC	AFL	IBM	NBC	OPEC
SAG	TRW	TWA	YMCA	

- Units of measurement also appear without the period except in abbreviations that spell regular words.

  yr   lb   m   tsp   tbsp   no.   in.

- Abbreviations that require periods should be typed without spaces between the periods and the letters.

  a.m.   p.m.   i.e.   pp.   etc.

- A single period should be used when an abbreviation ends a sentence. Any other punctuation would *follow* the abbreviation.

  The book was published in the U.S.A.

- Was the book published in the U.S.A.?

  If you plan on attending the meeting at 9 a.m., you will need to call Mr. Jones for instructions.

- Abbreviations should not begin a sentence unless they are never spelled out.

  Building 102 is going to be remodeled this summer.

  Not: Bldg. 102 is going to be remodeled this summer.

  OK: Mr. Abby is surpervising the renovation.

The following list serves as a quick reference for common abbreviations of words, phrases, and measurements.

Words and Phrases

bachelor of arts	A.B. or B.A.	end of month	e.o.m.
abbreviation	abbr.	and others	
automated data		(et alii)	et al.
processing	ADP	and the following	
before noon	a.m.	(et sequentia)	et seq.
approximately	approx.	and so forth	
avenue	Ave.	(et cetera)	etc.
building	Bldg.	and following	
boulevard	Blvd.	page, pages	f., ff.
buyer's option	b.o.	free on board	f.o.b.
cash before		general issue;	
delivery	c.b.d.	government	
company	Co.	issue	GI
cash on delivery	c.o.d.	gross national	
cost of living		product	GNP
adjustment	COLA	gross weight	gr. wt.
continued	con.	in the same place	
corporation	Corp.	(ibidem)	ibid.
certified public		the same (idem)	id.
accountant	C.P.A.	that is (id est)	i.e.
credit or creditor	cr.	I owe you	IOU
court	Ct.	intelligence	
		quotient	IQ
the same (ditto)	do.	junior	Jr.
debit or debtor	dr.	in the place cited	
doctor, drive	Dr.	(loco citato)	loc. cit.
east	E.	op. cit	
for example		limited	Ltd.
(exempli gratia)	e.g.		

lieutenant governor	Lt. Gov.
money supply	M_1, M_2
monsieur, messieurs	M., MM.
memorandum	memo
mademoiselle	Mlle.
madam, mesdames	Mme., Mmes.
month	mo.
mister (Messrs.)	Mr.
mistress	Mrs.
feminine title	Ms., Mses.
manuscript, manuscripts	MS., MSS.
north	N.
not available, not applicable	NA.
northeast	NE.
not elsewhere classified	n.e.c.
not elsewhere specified	n.e.s.
number, numbers	No., Nos.
northwest	NW.
okay	ok
in the work cited (opere citato)	op. cit.
public address system	PA
personal identification number	PIN
Place	Pl.
afternoon (post meridiem)	p.m.
post office box	P.O. Box

temporarily (pro tempore)	pro tem
postscript; public school (with number)	P.S.
random access memory	RAM
research and development	R&D
road	Rd.
reverend	Rev.
rural free delivery	R.F.D.
railroad	RR.
south	S.
savings and loan	S&L('s)
without date (sine die)	s.d.
southeast	SE.
second, third	2d, 3d
superhigh frequency	SHF
standard operating procedure	SOP
wireless distress signal	SOS
square, street	Sq.
senior	Sr.
street	St.
superintendent	Supt.
surgeon	Surg.
southwest	SW.
township, townships	T., Tps.
terrace	Ter.
television	TV
ultra high frequency	UHF
United States of America	U.S.A.

U.S. Army	USA	very important	
U.S. Highway	U.S. 10	person	VIP
No. 10	U.S. No. 10	west	W.
		without pay	w.o.p.
versus or against	v. or vs.		
video cassette re-		Zone Improvement	
corder	VCR	Plan	ZIP
very high frequency	VHF	9-digit ZIP Code	ZIP + 4

Units of Measurement

ampere	A	deka (prefix of ten)	da
atto (prefix one-		dekagram	dag
quintillionth)	a	dekaliter	daL
absolute	abs	dekameter	dam
alternating current	ac	square dekameter	dam^2
ampere-hour	Ah	cubic dekameter	dam^3
ampere per meter	A/m	decibel	dB
atomic weight	at wt	decibel unit	dBu
		direct current	dc
baud	Bd	decigram	dg
boiling point	bp	deciliter	dL
British thermal unit	Btu	dollar	dol
bushel	bu	dozen	doz
cent	c, c, or ct	electromagnetic	
centi (prefix of one-		unit	emu
hundredth)	c	erg	erg
degree Celcius	°C		
calorie	cal	Fahrenheit	F
centigram	cg	frequency modula-	
centiliter	cL	tion	FM
centimeter	cm	foot	ft
cycles per minute	c/m	square foot	ft^2
square centimenter	cm^2	cubic foot	ft^3
cubic centimeter	cm^3	conventional foot	
cubic feet	ft^3	of water	ftH$_2$O
cubic inches	in^3	foot-pound	ft.lb
		foot per minute	ft/min
day	d	square foot per	
deci (prefix of one		minute	f^2/min
tenth)	d	foot per second	ft/sec

square foot per second	f²/sec	square kilometer	km²
foot per second squared	ft/sec²	kilometer per hour	km/h
		knot (speed)	kn
		kilowatt	kW
		kilowatt-hour	kWh
giga (prefix of one billion)	G	liter	L
gram, acceleration of gravity	g	pound	lb
		pound-force	lbf
gallon	gal	pound-force foot	lbf/ft
gallons per minute	gal/min	low frequency	LF
gallons per second	gal/s	linear foot	lin ft
gram per cubic centimeter	g/cm³	lines per minute	l/m
		lines per second	l/s
gigahertz	GHz	liter per second	L/s
hour	h	mega (prefix of 1 million)	M
high frequency	HF	million (6 million)	M, 6M
hectogram	hg	meter	m
hectometer	hm	milli (prefix of one thousandth)	m
horsepower	hp		
horsepower-hour	hph	monetary aggregate	M
hertz (cycles per second)	Hz		
		square meter	m²
inside diameter	id	cubic meter	m³
indicated horsepower	ihp	micro (prefix of one millionth)	u
inch	in.	milliampere	mA
inch squared	in²	megacycle	Mc
inch per hour	in/h	milligram	mg
inch-pound	in-lb	microgram	ug
inch per second	in/s	megahertz	MHz
kelvin (degree symbol improper)	K	millihertz	mHz
thousand	k	mile	mi
kilogram	kg	square mile	mi²
kilometer	km	mile(s) per gallon	mi/gal
kilogram-force	kgf	mile per hour	mi/h
kilohertz	kHz	mil	mil
kilometer	km	minute (time)	min
		milliliter	mL

square milliliter	mL²	pint	pt
millimeter	mm	picowatt	pW
square millimeter	mm²	quart	qt
micrometer	um		
square micrometer	um²	revolutions per	
month	mo	minute	r/min
molecular weight	mol wt	root mean square	rms
melting point	mp	revolutions per	
millisecond	ms	second	r/s
microsecond	us		
megaton	Mt	second	s
millivolt	mV	shilling	s
microvolt	uV	second-foot	s-ft
megawatt	MW	standard cubic feet	
milliwatt	mW	(feet)	stdft³
microwatt	uW	trillion cubic feet	Tft³
megawatt-days per		tablespoonful	tbsp
ton	MWd/t	therm	thm
		ton	ton
nano	n	teaspoonful	tsp
nanosecond	ns		
		atomic mass unit	u
outside diameter	od	ultra high fre-	
ounce (avoirdupois)	oz	quency	UHF
pico (prefix of one		volt	V
trillionth)	p	voltampere	VA
Pascal	Pa	very high frequency	VHF
percent	pct	volt per meter	V/m
water-holding			
energy	pF	watt	W
hydrogen-ion		watt per meter	
concentration	pH	kelvin	W/(m·K)
peck	pk	yard	yd
parts per million	p/m	square yard	yd²
picosecond	ps	year	yr

• NUMBERS •

Cover the indented sentence below with your hand. Now remove it and quickly glance at the page.

In one thousand nine-hundred and sixty-nine, Neil Armstrong landed on the moon, ushering in the space age.

What caught your eye? "Neil Armstrong," most likely. But what about the date? Notice that numbers get lost when they are spelled out. Figures, on the other hand, provide readers with easy reference to critical points. In most business writing, use figures instead of spelled-out numbers for

- Weights and measures.
- Degrees of temperature.
- Dimensions.
- Decimals.
- Market quotations.
- Street numbers.
- Pages of books.
- Time of day.

For clarity, sometimes it's best to spell out numbers. A list of suggestions on when to spell out numbers follows. Spell out:

1. Numbers one to ten.
2. The shorter of two consecutive numbers.
3. Numbers that introduce a sentence.
4. Approximations.
5. Common fractions.
6. Million or billion.

• RESEARCH TOOLS FOR BUSINESS •

Guide to Book Reviews

Book Review Index. Detroit, Mich.: Gale Research Co., 1965 to present.

Guide to Periodicals

Applied Science and Technology Index. Bronx, N.Y.: H. W. Wilson Co., 1958 to present.

Business Periodicals Index. Bronx, N.Y.: H. W. Wilson Co., 1958 to present.

Accountants, Index. New York: American Institute of Certified Public Accountants, 1920 to present.

Guide to Newspapers

Bell & Howell Newspaper Index. Wooster, Ohio: Bell & Howell.
The Wall Street Journal Index. New York: Dow Jones & Co., 1958 to present.

Guide to Periodical Abstracts

Personnel Management Abstracts. Ann Arbor, Mich.: Graduate School of Business Administration, Division of Research, 1955 to present.
Computing Review. New York: Association for Computing Machinery, 1960 to present.

Guides to Government Documents

Android, John L. ed. *Guide to U.S. Government Publications.* McLean, Va.: Documents Index, 1981.
CIS/Index. Washington D.C.: Congressional Information Service, Inc., 1970 to present.
Federal Index. Cleveland, Ohio: Predicasts, Inc., 1977 to present.

Guides to Directories

Dun & Bradstreet, Inc. Million Dollar Directory. New York: Dun & Bradstreet, Inc., 1959 to present.
Standard & Poor's *Register of Corporations, Directors, and Executives.* New York: Standard & Poor's Corp., 1928 to present.

Guide to Investment Manuals

Moody's Manuals. New York: Moody's Investors Service, Inc.

Guide to Data Base Services

Bibliographic Retrieval Services (BRS)
1200 Route 7
Latham, NY 12110
DIALOG Information Retrieval Service
3460 Hillview Ave.
Palo Alto, CA 94304
LEXIS
Mead Data Control
9393 Springboro Pike
P.O. Box 933
Dayton, OH 45401

• FOLDING BUSINESS CORRESPONDENCE •

A reader's first impression of your business messages is crucial. That impression begins *before* the reader sees your words. The care with which you fold letters, for example, may influence the seriousness with which they are read.

We have all spotted "junk mail" by the careless, off-center overlap of the hurried fold. Avoid giving your important messages the look and feel of junk mail. Practice proper folding.

BUSINESS-SIZED ENVELOPE

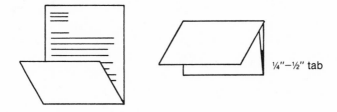

¼"–½" tab

Part Six

Sample Business Documents

• SHORT MEMO •

March 4, 198___

To: Beverly Whitworth

From: Clark Burton

Re: Inventory Levels

As you requested, here's a rundown of stock that needs to be reordered. You'll note that we still have many cameras; however, camera orders have increased lately, so we need more lead time for reordering.

Product	Quantity Left
Z180 Cameras	500
PL3 Pinhole Lense	15
T360 Scanner	50
R150 Controller	10
R25 Monitor	28

If you will initial this memo, I'll initiate a purchase requisition for these items. Please don't hesitate to ask me any questions regarding this matter.

cc: John Appleton
      Jill Canaby

• LONG MEMO (MEMO REPORT) •

To: Ron Becker

From: Stan Keaton

Date: January 10, 1986

Subject: Condor Project Publicity

Overview

Daniel Strider informed me about Clear Vision, Inc.'s involvement in the Condor Project. He has convinced me that we could get tremendous advertising mileage out of this project. Ads dramatizing the plight of the California Condor while giving a low-key plug for Clear Vision, Inc. could reap the following benefits:

- Instant recognition.
- Image enhancement.
- Goodwill.
- Memorability.
- Graphic oomph.
- Urgency/drama.
- Differentiation.

Ad Concept

Picture a Condor chick hatching in its nest at the San Diego Zoo. Above the copy reads something like this:

Sometimes the camera you choose. . . .

[Picture of Condor Chick]

can mean the difference between life and death.

Then, of course, the copy below would explain the use of EV3057IR cameras and Clear Vision, Inc. security systems in the fight to save the Condor. Low-key information on how to contact Excelcior's representatives would follow. The right-hand corner would be devoted to information about the Condor Project.

Benefits

Imagine the benefits of such an ad: The ad would mean instant recognition because the Condor Project garners national coverage. Not only would we get free press coverage, but people would *remember* Clear Vision, Inc.'s name through association with the project.

As for memorability, what could be more urgent, dramatic, and moving than the hatching of a newborn chick of an almost-extinct species? A subtle message explaining the importance of Clear Vision, Inc. security systems would really separate us from the competition.

Lastly, the ad would generate public goodwill because we would be *helping* the cause (and our own at the same time).

Conclusion

All of these reasons spell differentiation through advertising. We could use the differentiation strategy in advertising to gain industry-wide recognition.

If you will give the go-ahead, Daniel Strider and I will travel to the San Diego Zoo and obtain photographs for the ads. The Condor Project will give us our pick of rare photographs and footage.

Within two weeks I could have ten rough layouts for ads for you to choose. Daniel has envisioned choosing one memorable line and alternating photographs to create "graphic oomph." By changing the photos (but keeping the copy the same) people would continue to look at the ads. For little added cost we could have a host of new ads.

Daniel has certainly galvanized my support and enthusiasm for this project. If our plans meet with your approval, I could begin work on this project immediately.

cc: Daniel Strider
     Marsha Reynolds
     Douglas Finegold

• SALES LETTER •

DECADE SOUND TECHNOLOGIES, INC.
298 Third St.   Cincinnati, Ohio 98293   (322) 489-3892

September 3, 1986

Ms. Virginia Keller
Vice President of Sales
Technolog Discounts Sales, Inc.
13982 N.W. 40th Place
Belleview, WA 60293

Dear Ms. Keller:

Why are the editors of *Sound World, Record News,* and *Stereo Today* planning upcoming articles on Decade's revolutionary Series IV speakers?

Perhaps because they know a good thing. Consider what Series IV speakers offer your clientele:

- Unmatched performance in the 40–80 watt range.
- Compact size for today's efficient living environments.
- Stunning walnut cabinetry, handcrafted by Victors, Inc.

Now consider what Series IV offers you at Technolog Discounts:

- Profit potential of up to 120%, based on volume orders.
- A 50% savings in storage and display space, thanks to the compact design of Series IV speakers.
- Factory-backed warranties and service agreements that relieve Technolog Discounts of after-sales contacts.

We want you to see and hear the Series IV before *Sound World, Record News,* and *Stereo Today* spread the good word. Tom Mason, Northwest Technical Representative, will contact you before Friday, September 11, to make an appointment.

TECHNOLOG DISCOUNTS has led the retail stereo field for years by knowing more than the competition. We'd like you to know about Series IV.

Cordially,

Brett Almaster

Brett Almaster
Director of Marketing

• DIRECT SALES LETTER 1 •

WILSON COMPUTER SERVICES
88 North Evans St.   Phoenix, Arizona 85395   (872) 7680-1793

"The computers are down."

Have you said those words to customers lately? Business comes to a halt. Expensive personnel sit idle. Customers fume.

Wilson Computer Services offers fast, expert repair of virtually all micro- and mini-computers now in business use. Last year we serviced 8,200 computers *on site*, with an average repair time of less than 50 minutes. We offer you:

- Expert repairmen, each with factory certificates of training and at least three years experience in computer repair.
- Radio-dispatched vans for at-a-minute's-notice service.
- Warranties and bonds to guarantee quality workmanship.
- The best rates in the industry.

We would like to get to know you and your needs *before* a computer emergency arises. Please call Cheryl Sanders, Director of Marketing, for a free analysis by one of our repair staff of your service needs.

"The computers are up" at your company, with Wilson Computer Services on call.

Best wishes,

Nelson R. Tichner

Nelson R. Tichner
Vice President of Operations

• DIRECT SALES LETTER 2 •

Dear Marketer:

When specifying engineers recommend equipment, they turn to . . . *Machine Vision Buyers Directory* for the latest in solid state imaging products. Since you're selling to this growing market, MVBD offers a good opportunity to showcase your products.

The 1986 edition will have

- Bonus distribution at Nepcon, electronics' largest show.
- Twelve-month selling power for your ads and product releases.
- Editorials on image analysis, inspection, and microscopy.
- Reader inquiry cards for quick sales leads.
- The biggest circulation of any buying guide.

Please look over the enclosed 1985 edition. You'll notice that most of your major competitors have taken advantage of this opportunity. We're sure that you, too, would like a piece of the action.

Next week Cindy Anderson, our account executive, will contact you to answer any of your questions. For rates and additional information, refer to the enclosed information packet.

When you're ready to sell, let *Machine Vision Buyers Directory* do your talking.

Best wishes,

Maynard G. Ferguson

Maynard J. Ferguson
Publisher

MJF/win

Encl.

• CLAIMS (COMPLAINT) LETTER •

HENDERSON ASSOCIATES, INC.
324 Conway Plaza   Dallas, Texas 60403   (823) 873-2783

January 7, 1986

Ms. Sandra Matthews
Production Director
Franklin Publishers, Inc.
4982 Ninth St.
Milwaukee, Wisconsin 50304

Dear Ms. Matthews:

On July 6, 1985, we bought 500 copies of *The Training Guide* directly from your company. The salesperson involved was Mark Walker. He convinced us at the time that, in spite of the high price per book, we would find the *Guide* a valuable resource that could be used year after year.

By the first of this year, less than six months from the time of purchase, more than two thirds of books are unusable due to split spines. Many of the books have literally fallen into separate pieces. (I enclose a typical volume for your inspection.)

Henderson Associates have used these books on only three training occasions. At each, the books were treated with care and common sense. We are at a loss to explain why they are falling apart.

In any case, we insist that the damaged books (numbering 305 at last count) be replaced without charge to the company. You may wish to simply replace the entire lot of 500, assuming that the remaining whole books will also fall into premature disrepair.

It may be helpful for you to know that we are impressed with the content of the *Guide* and anticipate ordering more copies in the future once this unfortunate incident (perhaps the binder's mistake?) is satisfactorily resolved.

We ask that you contact Ralph Murray, our director of training, to make arrangements for the replacement.

Sincerely,

Gloria Vendersmith

Gloria Vendersmith
Vice President, External Projects

Enclosures: Damaged training guide from Franklin Publishers, Inc.

• ADJUSTMENT LETTER •

FRANKLIN PUBLISHERS, INC.
4982 Ninth St.   Milwaukee, Wisconsin 50304   (222) 323-1234

Ms Gloria Vendersmith
Vice President, External Projects
Henderson Associates, Inc.
324 Conway Plaza
Dallas, Texas 60403

Dear Ms. Vendersmith:

Thank you for your careful description of the broken bindings on some copies of *The Training Guide*. We deeply regret your inconvenience in this matter and wish to offer both an explanation and adjustment.

Approximately 700 copies of the book were subcontracted by our usual binder to a small press in Chicago. These books, as you have discovered, were improperly bound. But because they were indistinguishable in storage from properly bound copies, we were unable to recall them.

I have instructed Brenda Connell, our sales director, to contact Ralph Murray, as you instructed. Brenda will see that replacement copies are provided by express shipment without charge to your company.

We're pleased that you approve the content of the *Guide* and trust that this unfortunate mishap will not interrupt a business relationship we value.

Sincerely,

Sandra Matthews

Sandra Matthews
Production Director

• CREDIT APPROVAL LETTER •

November 30, 198—

Mr. Rubin Clayton
Operations Manager
Hamilton Suits Ltd.
145 Ami Boulevard
New York, NY 85968

Re: November 5 Credit Application

Dear Mr. Clayton:

Welcome to the La Jeunesse Fashion family for business executives climbing the corporate ladder. As a result of your considerable credit history, you've been extended a *$100,000 line of credit.*

As a preferred retailer, you're entitled to special discounts during Spring Clearance Sales and other special events. As with our other credit accounts, credit terms are:

- Net 30 days.
- Two percent "on-time" discount.
- FOB shipping point.

You may be interested to know that our Fall Fashion Catalog will be out in two weeks. As a preferred retailer, you'll receive a 15 percent discount on Le Jeunesse's L'Urbane designer suit line.

Once again, thank you for your interest in La Jeunesse Fashion. We look forward to doing business with you.

Sincerely,

Gerard Conoble

Gerard Conoble
Special Account Manager

GC/lj
Encls.

• CREDIT DENIAL LETTER •

January 22, 198__

Mr. Richard Sherwood
Purchasing Manager
Domestic Robots, Inc.
3535 N. Clark St.
Hampton, CA 54545

Dear Mr. Sherwood:

Thank you for applying for a Textron Plastics Preferred Customer Account. As this time, however, you do not qualify for a preferred customer account. In order to qualify, you need to

1. Establish credit history with banks and vendors.
2. Order more than 50 units every three months.

You're probably saying, "how can I *establish* credit when I can't pay on credit?" Well, we were in the same boat six years ago. May we suggest that you order on COD basis (check acceptable) for a while, and then resubmit your application in six months?

We see great possibilities in your fledgling business and hope to grow with you every step of the way. Let me know if you have any questions about our credit policy.

Textron Plastics truly hopes to count you among its preferred customers in the near future.

Sincerely,

Edmund J. Sherman

Edmund J. Sherman
Credit Manager

EJS/cd

• LETTER RESPONDING TO A PROBLEM •

January 22, 1986

Ms. Janice Watkins
Operations Manager
Millbrook Water Supply
77 Meadow Lane
Anaheim, CA 70231

Dear Ms. Watkins:

Your letter of January 17, 1986, came as a surprise to the company.

We apologize that you received partial shipments of containers on five separate occasions. After investigating the matter, we found that our driver had been diverting these containers for personal uses. To avert this problem, we have hired a new driver for your route.

Rest assured that Percy Container Corps will deliver your containers on time in the future. We know how important it is to have enough containers for your business.

If you encounter any difficulties, please don't hesitate to call me at (800) 773-1121.

Sincerely,

Ronald Johnson
Vice President Sales

• COLLECTION LETTER: FIRST NOTICE •

The following form could be attached to a copy of your customer's bill:

Just a reminder. . .

According to our records, your account is now past due in the amount of $87.00. If you've paid as of (date), we'd like to thank you.

If not, please send in your payment or let us hear from you by return mail or phone (Collection Department: [213] 888-1122).

Your business and friendship are important to us. We look forward to continuing this relationship.

Sincerely,

Excelsior Foods

Excelsior Foods

• RECOMMENDATION LETTER •

MARYMOUNT UNIVERSITY
324 Sheridan Road   Chicago, Illinois 60610   (312) 536-5478

January 26, 198—

Jackson Law School
2331 West Clark St.
Chicago, Il 60710

To the Admissions Committee:

It is my great pleasure to describe the personal and scholarly qualities of Mr. John Kisner as I have come to know them over the past year.

Mr. Kisner, who will be graduating this semester, is quite a scholar. For his fine work last semester, he received the highest "A" grade I have ever given. It's no wonder that his career at Marymount has been highlighted by excellent grades. Since transferring to this campus two years ago, he has a cumulative GPA of 3.9 out of 4.0—no small accomplishment.

As stated in his essay and resume, Mr. Kisner has been involved in many extracurricular activities, won awards, and has been a young leader in the Evanston community. Last semester, he was especially valuable to the classroom in his consistent ability to analyze situations and synthesize arguments with remarkable speed. Time and time again John's clear thinking—and I might add, superb writing abilities—earned him the highest marks in the class.

Mr. Kisner's other skills include word processing expertise, speech training, and a near-photographic memory. In addition, he is an accomplished pianist. In light of these and other skills, young Mr. Kisner's academic career takes on greater lustre.

Finally, since I have seen him on a twice-weekly basis over the past year, I'd like to mention that John is a joy to teach. He is mature about the ups and downs, the give-and-take, and the successes and disappointments of the classroom. He's level-headed, dedicated to the task at hand, and a joy to have as a student and fellow scholar.

If I can elaborate on these remarks, please do not hesitate to call me at Marymount University (312) 536-1212.

Robert C. Scanlon

Robert C. Scanlon
Professor, Business Communication

• RESIGNATION LETTER •

December 16, 1985

Mr. Robert Barnes
President
Warton Engineering, Inc.
242 South Coast Highway
San Clemente, CA 98283

Dear Bob,

After careful consideration, I have decided to resign from my position as Senior Engineer with Warton, effective January 1, 1986.

While it is not my purpose in this letter to rehearse the many factors I've considered, I do want you to know how valuable your support and counsel has been over the past eight years.

My current assignments will be completed by the effective date of my resignation. If you would like me to assist in the training of a replacement for my position, I will be happy to cooperate.

Again, my sincere thanks for your support, professional and personal, during my years at Warton.

Sincerely,

Wendell C. Collins

Wendell C. Collins
Senior Engineer

• INSTRUCTIONAL/PROCEDURAL WRITING: FOUR STEPS TO EARTHQUAKE SAFETY •

Will you know what to do when a major earthquake strikes during business hours?

Yes—thanks to your careful reading of this document and your common sense.

The Main Alarm—Your Signal of a Major Quake

The main alarm will sound when earthquake vibrations exceed Richter 4.0. Take the following actions immediately.

Your First Step.   Seek a safe place. Crouch under a desk or brace yourself in a doorway out of the path of falling debris.

Your Second Step.   Turn off emergency gas valves in your unit. These valves are marked with a large red "X" on the wall. Make sure you are physically safe before attempting to shut off the valves.

Your Third Step.   Lock all files in your unit. When the quake subsides, make sure all company file drawers and cases are locked before leaving your work area.

Your Fourth Step.   Leave your work area and assemble outside at your unit's designated meeting point. Supervisors will make sure all unit employees are accounted for.

If you or another worker is injured in an earthquake, dial the company's medic alert number, 999. Take first aid measures while awaiting the prompt response of paramedics.

Remember the four steps—"Personal safety, gas valves, lock files, leave"—in preparation for the company earthquake drills and actual temblars. As a lifesaving reminder, the four steps are printed in red above each fire extinguisher in the building.

• APPLICATION LETTER •

March 16, 1986

Mr. William Folkes
Director of Personnel
Harbor Insurance, Inc.
5892 Seaview Road
San Diego, CA 96829

Dear Mr. Folkes:

I am pleased to apply for the position of insurance saleman, as advertised in the March issue of *Insurance Monthly* (p. 127).

My resume (enclosed) sums up my qualifications for this position. You may find particular interest both in my academic preparation (seven courses in Marketing and Sales) and practical experience (a summer internship with John Hancock Insurance).

I would value the chance to meet with you in person to discuss our mutual goals. Please contact me at home (439-2934) after 4:00 P.M.

Sincerely,

Victor Ramirez

Victor Ramirez

• CHRONOLOGICAL RESUME •

JOEL M. SMITHSON
1342 Western Ave.
San Leandro, CA 93829
(415) 493-4902

CAREER GOAL
To begin as an entry level marketing specialist for ADAMS ENTERPRISES, INC.; with experience, to supervise projects in new product development.

EDUCATION
UNIVERSITY OF CALIFORNIA AT LOS ANGELES, B.A. (Marketing), May 1986.

Honors and Achievements:

- Dean's List four semesters.
- Senior Award for Business Potential.
- GPA 3.78 on 4-point scale.
- Colgate Scholarship, 1984–85.

Pertinent Coursework:
- Multinational Marketing.
- Marketing Logistics.
- Marketing Analysis and Strategy.
- Sales Force Management.
- Marketing Research.

EXPERIENCE
TRW, Credit Marketing Intern
Responsibilities: Assisted in the design and development of marketing strategies for consumer and business credit services. September 1984–May 1985.

CitiCorp Financial Services, Teller
Responsibilities: Handled cash, dealt with customers, assisted in training of new tellers. June 1982–August 1984

PERSONAL
BACKGROUND
I'm a 23-year-old self-starter who loves to travel. My hobbies include amateur astronomy, stamp collecting, and skiing. I have enjoyed serving on the Mayor's committee for disadvantaged youth since 1984.

References will be furnished upon request.

• FUNCTIONAL RESUME •

KATHLEEN SEVERS
2832 Westway Dr.
Miami, FL 60293
(392) 389-8928

EXPERIENCE IN THE MANAGEMENT OF
MARKETING CAMPAIGNS

Project Leader, FROZEN YOGURT LOVES AMERICA, INC. (FYLA), 1983-1984.

Supervised marketing of frozen yogurt to grocery chains in California, Oregon, Nevada, and Washington. In nine months, our unit contributed to an 85 percent increase in yogurt orders from chains.

Marketing Specialist, PERSONAL COMPUTER SALES, INC., 1982-1983.

Developed newspaper, radio, and television ads for microcomputers, software, and peripherals. Had sole responsibility for "Customer Hotline," a service offered to all purchasers of major systems.

Advertising Intern, PEABODY, SMITH, AND FENWICK AGENCY, 1981-1982.

Worked part-time during my senior year of college in the development of advertising programs for such clients as Star-Kist, Western Union, Nike, Campbell's Soup, and others. Learned layout and design skills from award-winning advertising executives.

EDUCATION FOR MARKETING MANAGEMENT

B.A. in Business Administration (Marketing emphasis), UNIVERSITY OF FLORIDA, June, 1982.

Dean's List five times.
Vice President, Student Marketing Association

Four summer seminars sponsored by the American Marketing Association (1979-1982).

PERSONAL QUALIFICATIONS FOR A CAREER IN MARKETING

I'm an outgoing, energetic person who enjoys meeting challenges. My interests include skiing, photography, and creative writing. I'm free to travel as the job requires.

Three or more professional and personal references will be provided upon request.

• PROGRESS REPORT ON DAVIDSON EMPLOYEE TRAINING PROGRAM

Summary of Work to Date

Under the terms of our contract signed January 7, 1985, Bertron Training Consultants have so far carried the development of an employee training project for Davidson, Inc., through the "approved concept" stage (refer to the "Milestones" chart on p. 8 of the Davidson proposal).

This report describes work undertaken to June 6, 1986, specifically the Initial Pilot Program stage of training development.

Description of Pilot Program

For a period of 60 days beginning March 8, 1986, and ending May 7, 1986, 42 Davidson employees participated in a one-hour-per-day pilot training program. Employees spent this hour in Training Facility 7, each working independently at microcomputers programmed for instruction in individualized skills development. All 42 employees completed the pilot program and participated in the pilot evaluation process.

Results of Evaluation

As can be judged from the data summaries appended to this report, employees felt the training process was very successful. Job productivity during the pilot program climbed 7 percent even though one hour from each workday was taken for training purposes. During the same period, absenteeism dropped 26 percent. Employees said they "looked forward to" and "couldn't wait for" the training sessions each day.

Problem Identification

In spite of the general success of the training program, some problems were identified for further development:

1. Program 1797 ("Final Wiring Inspection") has not been updated for 1986 changes in the Uniform Electric Code.
2. Program 863 ("Quality Control in Chip Installation") has a bug that terminates the program after the first seven minutes.

3. Program 9862 ("Team Techniques for Technical Writing") received a low rating by employees as too elementary for their practical needs.

Conclusion

Work continues to proceed according to contracted projections. Identified problems have been assigned to content specialists and programmers for correction. We will now move to the Implementation stage, with progress to be reported no later than August 6, 1986.

• FORMAT FOR THE LONG REPORT •

Letter of Transmittal

(A relatively brief letter, usually less than one page, directing the report to its intended audience, highlighting major findings, and thanking those involved in production.)

Cover

(The cover of the report often makes use of graphic enhancements. It should bear the title, author, date, and intended audience of the report.)

Abstract

(A statement, usually no longer than two or three paragraphs, summing up the report's contents, methods, and conclusions.)

Title Page

(A single page bearing the title of the report, the name of the person(s) writing the report, the name of the person(s) or organization(s) for whom the report is prepared, and any required documentation such as a research number. The date usually appears at the bottom of the title page.)

Preface or Foreword

(A brief treatment of background information, acknowledgement of contributors, references to other researchers, and appreciations.)

Table of Contents

(An alphanumeric outline of the report, usually with page numbers provided for major sections.)

List of Figures (or Tables or Maps)

(A list of figures or other features by order of appearance, with page numbers provided for each.)

Body

(The logical, ordered content of the report.)

Bibliography

(A list of references and citations, with full library information for each.)

Appendix

(A supplement for information that is not properly part of the report body.)

• OMNIFORM 3000 PROPOSAL •

submitted to

Mr. Vernon Edgar, President
Ms. Patricia Candlelary, Vice President
Mr. Arnold Bole, Technical Support

Excelsior Electronics, Inc.

by

David Hall
Technical Writer

Excelsior Electronics, Inc.

January 9, 198__

PROPOSAL OVERVIEW

This proposal examines the specific needs of the OMNI-FORM 3000 operator's manual and offers a unique approach to meet those needs effectively.

Since many documents begin with overview, what about using overviews in the OMNIFORM 3000 manual. Yes, but let's rename it. The word *overview* tells readers they're missing essential points—what's underneath the subject matter, or the "underview" so to speak. With an operator's manual almost as vast as the system itself, readers will want to "see" what they're "in for." What to do?

Give them the *OMNIVIEW,* a compartmentalized overview of what's in the chapter. (More about OMNIVIEWS later.) For now, here's an OMNIVIEW of this proposal:

```
NEEDS
  End user
  Image
MANUAL ANALYSIS
  Format
  Design
SPECIFICS
  Proposed Work
  Cost
  Time Frame
CONCLUSION
```

I. Special Needs—Excelsior and the End User

Before addressing format and design issues, let's consider the end user's needs and expectations and our objectives.

What do end users want? A lot of times they don't really know, but all readers have one thing in common. They want bite-sized information served on a silver platter. Likewise, the OMNI-FORM 3000 should be kept simple.

The best way to do this is to "compartmentalize." Just as computer circuits perform separate functions so should separate parts of the computer manual. No part should try to "do it all." Not only is the task impossible, but the reader would be hopelessly lost.

Even so, separate parts alone do not a computer manual make. These parts must be integrated. Related parts should be placed together, and the whole thing should be made compatible by using consistent form and language. Transitions such as an OMNIVIEW (more about OMNIVIEW, other transition methods, and compartmentalizing later) would accomplish this purpose.

What else spurs user interest? A humorous style often helps. Why humor? Because no matter how innovative the product, the average user will refuse to dredge through an uninspired computer manual. Readers regard book-size manuals as books and expect to be entertained, or they'll use the books as coasters. All of the truly interesting manuals—Applesoft's tutorial, for instance—make use of this device.

Now, let's turn to *Excelsior's* objectives. Of course, any operator's manual should introduce users to the system and educate them; but the OMNIFORM 3000 manual should also reflect the product image. Its tone should be Bold . . . Innovative . . . Exciting. . . . The manual should, with every ounce of conservative energy possible, exude these aspects by using action verbs and adjectives. With proper tone, users will "see" an exciting system with many desirable functions.

The next section examines ways to fulfill the user's needs and Excelsior's objectives in the OMNIFORM 3000 manual.

II. OMNIFORM Manual Analysis

This analysis will focus on format and design—in other words, "what to expect" and "how it will look."

Format. The format of written communication guides the reader through the material, no matter how complex. Thus, it's essential to compartmentalize by organizing, simplifying, and providing signposts for the reader. The OMNIFORM 3000 should be easy to read and interesting if the following issues are addressed:

- OMNIVIEW.
- Departments.
- Supporting material.
- Appendixes.
- Glossary.
- Titles.
- Blurbs.

1. OMNIVIEW

Each chapter should begin with an OMNIVIEW to give the user a quick snapshot of the contents. This serves two purposes: (1) to organize the material (compartmentalize) and (2) to reassure the reader that everything will be revealed one item at a time (bite-sized information).

The OMNIVIEW should not only list departments but also outline content. In addition, this feature will provide a keyword list referenced in the glossary (more about glossaries later).

2. Departments

As it stands now, the OMNIFORM manual's chapters play servant to too many masters. The installation section should be removed from each chapter and placed in an entire section in the back of the book. This would serve the purpose of compartmentalizing the book. Thus, readers won't be overwhelmed by too many topics in a chapter, yet they can refer to the same book for installation procedures.

The chapters also suffer from a confusing array of subheadings: specs, operational features, panel layout, operation, and installation to mention a few. In some chapters, operational features are listed under specs; in others, operational features enjoys separate status. To eliminate any confusion, the OMNIFORM 3000 chapters should have two main sections: Specifications and Operation. Specifications should come first so the user knows what the component is before operating it.

The Specifications heading can be further divided with these subheadings: hardware and operational features. Thus, both hard specs and features will be under the same roof though in separate compartments.

The Operation heading will provide just that: everything the user needs to know to operate the system.

Of course, given the needs of some chapters may differ slightly, this arrangement can be altered; but for most chapters, this system should be implemented.

3. Supporting Material

Wherever possible, the OMNIFORM 3000 material should be tied into checklists, examples, and illustrative material. Simple line drawings, an OMNIFORM operation anecdote, and a quick checklist should provide a good supporting cast to the content. Of course, complex drawings and those referred to in the installation section should be placed in appendixes.

4. Appendixes

Most of the complex drawings should remain in the appendixes; however, some drawings such as the one in Appendix A really belong within the confines of the chapter. Also, whenever possible, appendix charts and graphs should be used.

5. Glossary

Computer nomenclature holds its rightful place here. Words the average user wouldn't know should be defined in the glossary. The first time jargon appears in a chapter, it should be italicized, placed in the keyword list in the OMNIVIEW, and referenced to the glossary.

6. Titles

Now comes the fun part: writing easily remembered signposts or titles. If you please, chapter titles can be jazzed up to reflect the excitement of the system; for instance, underneath the chapter 2 heading, "JO-3000 Central Computer," the nickname "BIG JO" could appear. Or, hearkening back to a phrase everyone remembers from the *Wizard of Oz,* this subtitle could appear: "The Great and Powerful OMNIFORM."

Innovative language and a touch of whimsy or humor should inspire the user to read on. . . .

7. Blurbs

Humor can also be used in little blurbs (one per chapter) in the white space at column-side.

Whimsical anecdotes or blurbs should always be placed on the side. That way, readers can choose whether to pause for a breather.

Design. The OMNIFORM 3000 has the competition beat when it comes to systems innovation, capability, and software, and the reason is simple: innovation. Likewise, a little conservative innovation can go a long way toward upholding the product image. This section examines "the look" of the page and covers the following topics:

- Layout.
- Typeface.
- Color coding.
- Binding.
- Cover.

1. Layout

The OMNIFORM 3000 manual should have an expansive look. The system is expansive, and every page element should reflect that aspect. The layout ingredients look something like this:

a. Nine picas white space left side column.
b. Fifteen picas white space right side.
c. Twenty-seven picas column width.
d. One and a half picas column leading.
e. Nine picas margin top and bottom.

Whenever possible, pictures, drawings, and other graphics should liven the page.

2. Typeface

Choosing proper typeface can enhance readability. Often carelessly chosen, manual printers unwittingly provide road blocks to the user. Again, the goal is to simplify, organize, and provide the proper signposts to the reader. Studies have shown that using Serif typeface (typeface with rabbit ears) increases reading comprehension and speed. In addition, the type face should reflect the innovative OMNIFORM system.

For these reasons, the OMNIFORM 3000 manual should be typeset in Tiffany Medium or a similar typeface.

3. Color Coding

Inset color coded tabs (dictionary style) should be printed on the right-hand side indicating major headings such as Operation, Installation, Glossary, Appendixes, etc. These make it easier for the user to find major areas and sense the proportions of the manual.

4. Binding

Definitely loose leaf spiral. That way, users can add amendments as the system changes.

5. Cover

The OMNIFORM 3000 cover should be in color. Covers are to books as cereal boxes are to cereal. Whether a book or manual gets read often depends on its cover. Though you can't judge a book by its cover, you can certainly tell if it *looks* attractive. In addition, the cover should have pockets for revision logs. Therefore, budgets willing, the manual calls for a bold, innovative, colorful cover with pockets.

Recommendation: Use a two-color photo of Einstein's bust. Superimpose the OMNIFORM system and simple title "Operator's Manual." Then, below the picture at the bottom of the manual add this kicker:

OMNIFORM 3000

"Light years ahead of its time"

III. Proposal Specifics

This section covers proposed work, cost, and time schedules.

Proposed Work.   As an independent contractor, I would provide the following services:

1. Rewrite of the Omniform 3000 Manual and Table of Contents.
2. Generate material described in

- OMNIVIEW.
- Departments.
- Glossary.
- Titles.
- Blurbs.

3. Typeset all materials based on proposal recommendations or your specifications.

All Appendix artwork, graphics, line drawings, and photographs to be supplied by Excelsior. At your request, I can assemble all illustrative material for you at cost plus allowance for my time.

COST	
Rewrite of OMNIFORM 3000 manual, including departments	$12,000
OMNIVIEW, including keylist	500
Glossary, covering 130 pages	2,000
	$14,500

Typesetting costs to be determined (approximately $3,500), but I will charge cost. Any additional chapters or other material will be charged at the above rate. Also, additional rewrites will be charged accordingly.

Time Frame.   From the date you accept this proposal, the literature will be ready for typesetting in eight weeks or sooner.

IV. Conclusion

Besides the ideas mentioned in this proposal, there are three other advantages to hiring an in-house consultant: (1) immediate progress reports, (2) accessibility, and (3) control over the project. More importantly, I work on a Kaypro and have one at home. Thus, all I would need is a copy of the OMNIFORM 3000 manual disk, giving me a huge head start over outside consultants.

I trust that you have found this proposal helpful in planning for the OMNIFORM 3000 manual and look forward to working with you on this project. Thank you for the opportunity to submit this proposal.

• DETAILED COST PRESENTATION IN PROPOSALS •

Funding Requirements

Other headings could be used such as Financial Needs, Summary of Project Costs, and Estimated Budget. You may interchange the words to create a term suitable to your own needs.

Equipment

Teleconference equipment:		
Microphones	AA	
Speakers	BB	
Front Camera	CC	
Document Camera	DD	
NTSC CRT Display	EE	
Control Console	FF	
High-Resolution CRT Display	GG	
Scanner	HH	
Printer	II	
Control Console	JJ	
Total cost of teleconference equipment		$250,000

Conference room equipment:		
Tables	$1,230	
Chairs	655	
Curtains	220	
Carpeting	825	
Fixtures	330	
Pictures, frames	210	
Wall map of company locations	120	
Miscellaneous (ashtrays, plants, etc.)	60	
Total cost of room equipment		3,650
Total cost of all equipment		$253,650

Labor	*Hours*	*Rate*	*Extension*	
Department labor:				
Project manager	80	$20	$1,600	
Purchasing agent	30	12	360	
Contracted labor:				
Electrician	60	18	1,080	
Video technician	30	25	750	
Craftsmen	—	—	500	
Total cost of all labor				$4,290

Indirect Costs

Overhead

Indirect labor:		
Janatorial Cleanup	$30	
Secretarial Tasks	120	
Indirect material:		
Supplies used in construction	30	
Lighting, heat	90	
Total indirect costs		$270
Total funds needed for project		$258,210

• SHORT REPORT •

• MARKETING'S EFFECT ON THE PROFITABILITY OF SIR TOTTENHAM ROBOTS •

Prepared for

Ms. Elsinore Crandall, President
Chancellor Robots, Inc.
8675 Sherandon Avenue
Los Angeles, CA 97821

Prepared by

Jack Van de Weigh
Marketing Consultants, Inc.
228 West Schiller Av.
Chicago, Il 60093

January 22, 198__

Overview

This report shows that marketing has had a dramatic effect on the sales and promotion of Sir Tottenham Robots. In addition, it highlights a few trouble spots and offers suggestions for improvement.

Prior to management's decision to wage an "all-out" marketing blitz, the robot line was costing the company millions of dollars. Since then, the robot has made a remarkable recovery. Though not yet a profit maker, our survey suggests that it promises great profits in the future.

To analyze marketing's effect on Sir Tottenham Robots, the following profit equation was used:

Brand awareness + Perceived quality + Perceived value = Profitability

Given this equation, this report analyzes marketing's effect on each component of profitability.

Brand Awareness

This all-important category results from media advertising. Before the company started to advertise, its product was virtually unknown. Of course, the whole market had not yet been discovered by the consumer.

Fortunately, when Sir Tottenham Robots entered the market, no IBM-type companies occupied it. Except for a few small-time manufacturers, the market was virtually nonexistent.

Since then, Excelsior has made great strides to educate customers about the product. So that customers wouldn't be turned off by it's high-tech programming and sophistication, it was positioned as the

> "smart butler robot . . .
> only much, much more."

The ad went on to say how Sir Tottenham has a built-in vacuum and a number of other appliances. *Our market survey* suggests that with one fell swoop Excelsior linked itself to trustworthy servants and easy-to-use appliances.

When asked to respond to the question, "In one word, how would you describe this product?" These three responses were the most prevalent: smart, easy-to-use, and dependable. It's no wonder. They're the same words all the media and TV advertising used.

The following chart traces brand awareness in relation to media and television advertising and direct mailer purchases:

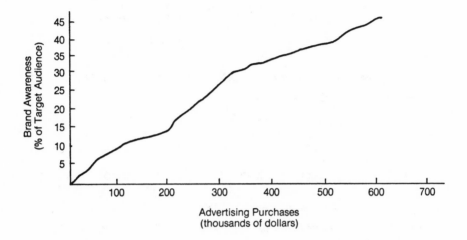

As the chart clearly shows, increased advertising in the form of print media and television advertising and direct mailers results in increased product awareness.

When our survey readers were asked how they knew about Sir Tottenham, two thirds replied television, one sixth replied magazines, and one sixth replied from direct mailers. Astoundingly, these ratios mirror Excelsior's proportional investment in each.

Perceived Quality

In this category, Sir Tottenham scored highest. Apparently America has a fascination with British butlers. Choosing the name "Sir Tottenham," giving him a British accent, and advertising him as smart, fastidious, and dedicated all contributed to consumers' high opinion.

In addition, as a result of the company's free comparison/trial use program, the robot scored high marks on reliability. Not only that, but people found the robot remarkably easy to use due to its ability to program itself based on voice commands.

The following bar graph compares Sir Tottenham's quality to the two other robot lines on the market:

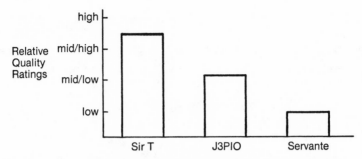

For those who responded that they found Sir Tottenham the best, we asked why. Here's the breakdown:

Trial comparison	25%
Name recognition	65
Didn't know	10

The conclusion can be drawn that perceptions of quality are largely due to advertising and trial/comparison use. The 25 percent becomes significant in light of the fact that the trial/comparison program has only existed for ten months, eight fewer than the advertising campaign.

Perceived Value

Once you've established perceived quality (preference), then customers will buy if (1) they have the need (2) they're comfortable with the price.

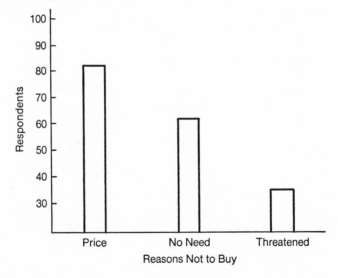

Here's where Sir Tottenham needs some work. As the graph on page 188 shows, of the 200 respondents who said they liked the product but would not buy it, 83 complained about the price (approximately $1,800).

Surprisingly, the other respondents said they had no need for the product or that their spouse might feel threatened by "someone" taking over the household tasks.

Here's where marketing hasn't really sold many potential customers. The advertising campaign must address these two issues and refute them with plausible arguements. Here's two suggestions:

1. **Price.** Ask the customer to compare the cost of Sir Tottenham to the cost of a cleaning person for one year. Or ask the customers to calculate the hours they spend vacuuming, doing the laundry, gardening, taking out the garbage, dusting, and cleaning each year and multiply it by five dollars. Then they can compare costs.
2. **Threat.** Ask consumers to think of Sir Tottenham as any other appliance, not as a member of the household. Also, ask them to think of Sir Tottenham as a liberator, not a usurper of household tasks.

Profitability

Revenue from the Sir Tottenham line has increased steadily whereas costs have actually declined per unit due to economies of scale. According to our survey, brand awareness and perceived quality have had a lot to do with these improvements. Note the revenue and cost graphs below and on page 190:

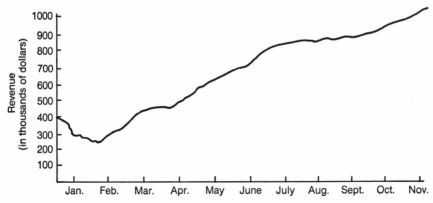

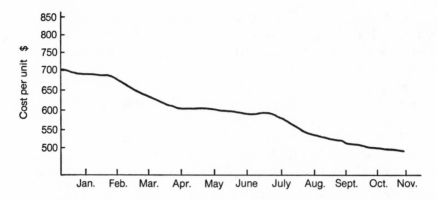

Except for an aberration during February, revenues have increased and costs have steadily decreased. If this trend continues, and there's no reason to believe it won't, Sir Tottenham Robots should be profitable within six months.

Conclusion

Sir Tottenham Robots shows remarkable strength in two out of the three components needed for increased sales: brand awareness and perceived quality. So far, however, the marketing campaign has failed to convince the customers of Sir Tottenham's value.

We recommend two courses of action:

1. Maintain expenditures on advertising/direct mailers and comparison/trial use campaigns to help maintain product awareness and perceived quality.
2. Allot new funds for a TV ad campaign that addresses the "needs" issue.

With just a little more marketing effort, the outlook appears very rosy, indeed, for Sir Tottenham Robots.

INDEX

A

Abbreviations, standard, 240–46
Accept, except, 137
Active memory, use of, 11–13
Ad hominem argumentation, 25
Adjustment letter
  recipe for, 96–97
  sample of, 160
Affect, effect, 137
Agreement, verbs, nouns, and pronouns,
  130–131
All right, alright, 137
All together, altogether, 138
Among, between, 138
Amount, number, 138
Antecedents, and pronouns, 129–130
Anxious, eager, 138
Apostrophes, use of, 126–127
Application letter
  recipe for, 95
  sample of, 168
Appositives, and dashes, 123
Artistic works, and capitalization, 128–129
Assembling words, 16
Association, as memory aid, 12

B

Between, among, 138
Blue style words, 57
Book reviews, guide to, 147
Bottom line statements, 50–51
Brevity, value of, 66–68
Business correspondence, folding, 148–49
Business document samples
  adjustment letter, 160
  application letter, 168
  chronological resumé, 169
  claims (complaint) letter, 159
  collection letter, 164
  credit approval letter, 161
  credit denial letter, 162
  direct sales letter, 157–58

Business document samples—Cont.
  functional resumé, 170
  instructional/procedural writing, 167
  long memo, 154–55
  long report format, 172
  memos, 153–55
  problem response letter, 163
  progress report, 171–72
  proposal, 172–82
  recommendation letter, 165
  reports, 171–73, 182–88
  resignation letter, 166
  resumé, 169–70
  sales letter, 156
  short memo, 153
  short report, 182–88

C

Capitalization, 128–29
Checklist for evaluation, 118
Choosing a style, 58
Choosing words, 48–49
Chronological resumé sample, 169
Claims (complaint) letter sample, 159
Claims letter recipe, 96
Collection letter
  recipe for, 97
  sample of, 164
Colons, use of, 122-24
Coloring words, 54–57
Commas, use of, 121, 124
Complement, compliment, 138
Compound antecedents, and pronouns, 130
Confused words, 137–40
Continual, continuous, 138
Contractions, and apostrophes, 127
Creating package, 90
Creating resume, 104–6
Credible, creditable, 139
Credit approval letter sample, 161
Credit denial letter sample, 162
Critical view of writing, 111–112
Cues for readers, 46–47

D

DALLAS approach to topics, 18
Dashes, use of, 123–24
Data base services, guide to, 148
Declaration of Independence, business
    writers, 5
Directories, guide to, 148
Direct quotations, and quotation marks, 125
Direct sales letter samples, 157–58
Disinterested, uninterested, 139
Documentation, source, 59
Documents
    brevity and, 66–69
    checklist for evaluating, 118
    choice of, 26–27
    form, 29
    mapping, 46–47
    organizing, 34–36
    presentation of, 98
    samples; see Business documents samples
    shaping, 37
    source documentation, 59

E

Each other, one another, 139
Eager, anxious, 138
Early message transmission, 41, 113
Editing
    for others, 99–100
    rapid, 64–65
Editors, and drafting process, 30
Effect, affect, 137
Electronic mail, writing for, 113–114
Eminent, imminent, 139
Evaluation checklist, 118
Except, accept, 137

F

Farther, further, 139
Feedback, 109–10
Figures, use of with numbers, 147
First draft, 33
First word, and capitalization, 128
Folding business correspondence, 148–49
Following, preceding, 139–40
Format cues, 46
Form documents, 29
Functional resumé sample, 170

G

Government documents, guide to, 148
Graphics, use of, 88–89
Grouping/organization, as memory aid, 12

H-I

Heavy noun reduction, 70
Idea production, 14–15
Imagery, as memory aid, 12
Imminent, eminent, 139
imprinting message, 83–84
In, into, 140
Indefinite pronoun antecedents, 130
Indefinite pronouns, and agreement, 131
Infer, imply, 140
Instructional/procedure writing sample, 167
Investment manuals, guide to, 148
Italics, use of, 125–26
Its, it's, 140

K-L

Key points relationships, 43–44
Keys to better spelling, 131–134
Lard reduction, 42
Letter organization, 94–97
Lie, lay, 140
Logical flaws, prevention of, 24–25
Long report format, 172–73

M

Mapping documents, 46–47
Measurements abbreviations, 144–46
Memory aids, 11–13
Memos, samples of short and long, 153–55
Memo writing, 93
ME perspective, 28
Message
    early transmission of, 41, 113
    imprinting, 83–84
    personalizing, 87, 113
Misplaced modifiers, 129
Misspelled words, list of, 133–34
Mnemonic devices/language, as memory
    aids, 13

N

Names, and capitalization, 128–29
Naturalness, importance of, 21–23
Needs, reader's, and letters, 94–95
Negative responses, 101–2
Newspapers, guide to, 148
Nouns, 70–71
Nudge, and writer's block, 9–10
Number, amount, 138
Numbers, use of figures and spelled out, 147

O

Objective case, and pronouns, 130
One another, each other, 139

Orange style words, 56
Organization
    of documents, 34–36
    letters, 94–97
    visual, 81–82
Outlining, 19–20

P

Package creation, 90
Paragraph planning, 38–40
Parentheses, use of, 123–24
Passive verbs, activation of, 74–75
Periodical abstracts, guide to, 148
Periodicals, guide to, 147
Personalizing messages, 87, 113
Personal presentation, documents, 98
Phrases and words abbreviations, 142–44
Plural antecedents, and pronouns, 129
Plural possessive, and apostrophe, 126
Plurals, chart of unusual, 135–36
Possessives, and apostrophes, 126–27
Post hoc ergo propter hoc logical error, 24
Preceding, following, 139–40
Presenting documents, 98
Prior feedback, 109
Problem response letter sample, 163
Problem statements, conversion of topics to, 18
Progress report sample, 171–72
Pronouns, 129–31
Proper nouns, and capitalization, 128
Proposal writing, 173–82
Punctuation
    apostrophes, 126–28
    colons, 122–24
    commas, 121, 124
    dashes, 123–24
    parentheses, 123–24
    quotation marks, 125
    semicolons, 121–22, 124
Purpose for writing, 17

Q–R

Quotation marks, use of, 125
Reader's needs, letters and, 94–95
Reading as aid to writing, 103
Recipient feedback, 109–10
Recommendation letter
    recipe for, 95
    sample of, 165
Red style words, 55
Repetitive rhythm, sentences, 78
Reports, format and samples, 171–73, 102–88
Research sources, 147–48

Resignation letter sample, 166
Restating obvious, logical error, 24
Resumé
    chronological sample, 169
    creation of, 104–6
    functional sample, 170
Revision, testing for, 63

S

Sales letter
    recipe for, 94–95
    samples of, 156–58
Samples of writing; see Business documents samples
Semicolons, use of, 121–22, 124
Senses, writing for, 107–8
Sentence variation, 78–80
Sexual bias, avoidance of, 85–86
Shaping documents, 37
Short report sample, 182–88
Short words and sentences, value of, 42
Single possessive, and apostrophe, 126
Singular antecedents, and pronouns, 129
Source documentation, 59
Spatial ordering, as memory aid, 12
Special accompaniments, documents, 98
Special mail presentation, documents, 98
Special plurals, and apostrophes, 127
Spelled-out numbers, 147
Spelling, 131–34
Standard abbreviations, 140–46
Straw man, logical error, 25
Strong verbs, 72–73
Style, choice of, 58
Style words, 55–57
Subjective case, and pronouns, 130
Subordinate information, 52–53
Summaries, importance of, 50–51

T

Team writing, 116–17
Testing for revision, 63
Third parties, and document presentation, 98
Titles, and italics, 126, 128–29
Topics, conversion to problem statements, 18
Transition signals, 45

U

Undistributed middle, logical error, 25
Uninterested, disinterested, 139
Units of measurements abbreviations, 144–46
Unusual plurals, chart of, 135–36

V

Variety in sentences, 78–80
Verbs, strong and passive, 72–75
Visual and verbal cues, 46–47
Visual organization, 81–82

W

Which, avoidance of, 76–77
Who or whom, 130
Word processor writing, 115
Words
  assembling, 16
  choice of, 48–49
  coloring, 54–57
  frequently confused words, 137–40

Words—*Cont.*
  list of misspelled, 133–34
  and phrases abbreviations, 142–44
Writer's block, 6–10
Writing
  purpose of, 17
  samples of; *see* Business documents
    samples
  for senses, 107–8
  with word processor, 115

Y

Yellow style words, 56
YOU perspective, 28
Your, you're, 140